I've just finished spending the day with Terri Broome. We've never met but I read her book and now I know her. Her book, *The Ordinary Road*, is a slice of life with all of its messiness, sin, joy, laughter, celebration and pain.... and Jesus. With refreshing authenticity (most writers are never this honest), a delightful conversational style (I felt as if we were talking across a cup of coffee), a profound understanding of Scripture (It's rare to encounter a writer who takes the Bible this seriously,) and an unbelievable determination to follow Jesus (He has to be careful what he says to her, because she'll do it)... she opens the doors of her life and invites the reader to listen to her stories. As I read her stories, I heard the "soft sound of sandaled feet" and my cynicism was met with the reality of a God who is loving... and loving all the time. Read this book and then give it to your friends. Both you and your friends will "rise up and call Terri Broome blessed."

STEVE BROWN,
professor at Reformed Theological Seminary in Orlando,
an author and the teacher on the syndicated teaching program, *Key Life.*

I've never known a clearer vessel of God's grace than the author of this soul-challenging book. Having learned to truly trust God by opening my hands to whatever He takes or gives has become one of the greatest freedoms my Christian life has known. And I didn't learn it in Bible College or on the mission field. I learned it from Terri. She is the Corrie ten Boom of this generation. Drink deeply.

RACHEL LEE CARTER
Christian Conference Speaker and Author,
Fashioned by Faith (Thomas Nelson.)

The Ordinary Road

Where Faith Became Sight

Short Stories By

Terri Broome

CrossBooks™
A Division of LifeWay
1663 Liberty Drive
Bloomington, IN 47403
www.crossbooks.com
Phone: 1-866-879-0502

First published by CrossBooks 07/30/2013

ISBN: 978-1-4627-2931-9 (sc)
ISBN: 978-1-4627-2933-3 (hc)
ISBN: 978-1-4627-2932-6 (e)

Library of Congress Control Number: 2013911639

Printed in the United States of America.

Dedicated to Vickie Vaughan. Love you more...

Let this be written for
a future generation that
a people not yet created
may praise the Lord.
Psalm 102:18

ACKNOWLEDGEMENTS

I would like to thank Todd Messer for the beautiful design of my cover. God gave me a vision and He took your creativity and breathed life into it. I am forever grateful.

Also, thank you to Jane Caldwell, Robin Ringley, Erin Sipe, Vickie Vaughan and Katherine Pasour for painstakingly reading over this manuscript. I know it was a labor of love. It has truly taken a village to make Terri a writer. I love you all.

TABLE OF CONTENTS

A Note

. . . to warn you that I am not a writer. I'm a wife and mother who feels most at home doing dishes and scrubbing toilets. I am an ordinary woman who knows the extraordinary God of the universe. Wow! Sometimes I want to pinch myself as I think about that fact. I will never take for granted that I get to talk to Him every day—and more importantly, that He talks to me.

I have many stories of God's love and faithfulness in my life and the lives of my family and friends, which I will be recounting in this book. Over the years, people have encouraged me to write my stories, telling me that they would make a great book. So I would write one here and there, but the truth is that my heart really wasn't in it. You see, I think that there are enough books on Christianity already published that sometimes keep people from reading the only book that really matters—the Bible. In fact, I've often said that if I ever did write a book, I would put, "Read your Bible" on every page. I have had the adventure of my life in that Book. Every time I open it, every time **you** open it, we are looking at the face of God. That thrills me!

On October 20, 2009, I asked God if He wanted me to write a book. I had to teach an exercise class that morning, which meant that my morning devotional time had to end no later than 7:30 a.m., or I'd be late. I looked at the clock, and it was 7:29. I thought I would read one more Psalm (I read straight through the Bible, and I happened to be in the Book of Psalms at the time), and what I read next made my heart start pounding.

> ***"Let this be written for a future generation, that a people not yet created may praise the Lord"*** (Psalm 102:18).

I went into the den to share this with my husband, and he said, "Do it!"

In earnest, I started almost immediately. Upon sharing one of the stories I was very proud of with my husband, he said the story was wonderful, but "That first paragraph is abominable."

We laughed our heads off, and I said, "It's a rough draft," (knowing the final draft might not be much better). I write exactly like I speak.

The next day, I was thinking maybe I could write all my stories down and then a **real** writer could make them sound wonderful and polished. Somehow, I felt God speak to my heart that He wanted me to write them just like I speak because they are **my** stories, and He does not necessarily want polished and perfect. He wants real. He helped me take off my "perfect" mask many years ago, and I am comfortable with all my flaws (they are part of the human condition, and God has used them to humble me and help me have compassion with others and their flaws). In this book, as in my everyday life, I will be painfully honest about myself and my walk with God. I am able to do this because I have stood in His presence completely undressed (spiritually speaking) and handed my naked "self" over to Him. I have found that He loves me exactly as I am, and because of that realization, I am no longer a slave to other people's opinions, although I do love people so much. I'm free because "Where the Spirit of the Lord is . . . there is freedom."

The day this writing endeavor began, I read the following from the devotional Streams in the Desert by L.B. Cowman (1965). God's timing is perfect.

"**N**ot of the Extraordinary"

"Now Moses kept the flock of Jethro his father-in-law, the priest of Midian; and he led the flock to the backside of the desert, and came to the mountain of God, even to Horeb. And the angel of the Lord appeared unto him in a flame of fire out of the midst of a bush" (Exodus 3:1-2).

> *"The vision came in the midst of common toil, and that is where the Lord delights to give His revelations. He seeks a man who is on the ordinary road, and the Divine fire leaps out at his feet. The mystic ladder can rise from the market place to Heaven. It can connect the realm of drudgery with the realms of grace.*

My Father God, help me to expect Thee on the ordinary road. I do not ask for sensational happenings. Commune with me through ordinary work and duty. Be my Companion when I take the common journey. Let the humble life be transfigured by Thy presence.

Some Christians think they must be always up to mounts of extraordinary joy and revelation; this is not after God's method. Those spiritual visits to high places, and that wonderful intercourse with the unseen world, are not in the promises; the daily life of communion is. And it is enough. We shall have the exceptional revelation if it be right for us.

There were but three disciples allowed to see the transfiguration, and those three entered the gloom of Gethsemane. No one can stay on the mount of privilege. There are duties in the valley. Christ found His lifework, not in the glory, but in the valley and was there truly and fully the Messiah. The value of the vision and glory is but their gift of fitness for work and endurance." (October 22nd devotional)

My Story

God found me at the age of twenty-two married, divorced, and on the verge of marrying again. How I got to that point is what this story is about. The God-shaped void in me had become so large that I couldn't control myself anymore, even though it was costing me what, at the time, was my most prized possession: a good reputation. Mind you, I am talking about a good reputation, not good character. There **is** a difference.

As a young adult, I could size up any crowd and quickly figure out just who I needed to be in order to fit in, and then deliver the person they would approve of. I guarded very closely my real "face," so people saw whatever face I thought they wanted to see. At that time, I couldn't have told you exactly what it was I was doing because that behavior was normal for me.

Over time, God has opened these truths to me as He knew I could bear to face them. If He had dumped all the truth on me that I now know all at one time, I guess it would have killed me. I love that I can now look at who I was and who I now am and be completely honest and open about it. God has enabled me to never give up on anyone else. I know the power of God firsthand, and I believe my life is a testament to the fact that no one is too hard for God to make righteous. Notice I didn't use the word ***good*** to describe what God makes us. He does something far better. "God made Him who had no sin to be sin for us, so that in Him we might become the ***righteousness*** of God" (2 Corinthians 5:21).

I married my dear husband, Rick, when I was only twenty-one and thought that he was going to fulfill me and the gnawing unrest in my soul would finally hush. Poor soul, he did not know what he was getting into, but it did not take long for him to realize that he had a tiger by the tail! He couldn't please me, and I was sure it was his fault. I remember lying beside him in bed and feeling so desperately lonely, when I had thought that lying next to him each night would give me all the love and security that I knew would make me happy.

I had never known anyone like Rick and didn't know the jewel I had. Because I was self-centered, manipulative, shallow, and deceptive, I just assumed that everyone else was too. We can only judge others by what is in our own hearts.

I know Rick is a sinner—saved by grace—because the Bible plainly says we all are, but I've never known anyone so naturally pure of heart as he is. He doesn't even know how to wear a "face;" he is just who he is.

Although Rick was trustworthy, I didn't trust him. Although he loved me very deeply, I didn't believe him. I treated him as if he was guilty of all the things I was. As I look back now, I'm glad God is merciful and loving, because if I had to watch someone hurt Rick the way I did, I'm not sure I would have let them live.

After Rick and I got married, I moved to Knoxville with him, and my unrest started at once. It didn't take me long to feel like I'd made a big mistake. I just wasn't happy in Knoxville, so we moved back to Johnson City. Are you surprised to learn I was not happy there, either? Since I was not happy no matter where we lived, I figured Rick must be the obvious reason. I did not want to hurt him or damage my prized reputation, so I stayed married as long as I could: about a year and a half. Of course, when I left, I made him out to be the bad guy, and everyone believed me. I was even able to completely convince myself. After all, I had to be able to live in my own skin, so self-deception had become my best friend. And due to my bubbly and outgoing personality, it was easy to get people to take my side.

Almost immediately, I got involved with someone else, and it turned serious quickly. Again, I thought the vacuum inside me would be filled by this new man. He took drugs and drank quite a bit. Under the influence of drugs and alcohol, he started talking to me about God, Satan, and hell. He started asking me all kinds of questions about what kind of person I had been. Naturally, I went into my innocent act, but he saw right through it since he was an even bigger player than me. He would not stop asking until I told him just about everything I had ever done. I was mortified at what I heard coming out of my mouth, and I crumbled under the weight of the realization of the truth. I had kept my life so exciting, busy, and superficial that I had never taken the time to really think about what kind of person I was and had been. I knew that I was going to hell and I deserved it. I was terrified.

I knew very little about church and most of the religious people I knew were very sincere, but not a lot of fun. Women were not allowed to wear jewelry, pants, or make-up, and they all had to have long hair. Dancing was against the rules, too! Unfortunately, that summed up just about everything I loved! However, under the conviction of the Holy Spirit, I came to the point of being willing to follow all those rules if God would just somehow come and rescue me from my sin.

One night in October 1988, I went outside to sit by myself because the guy I was dating was inside doing cocaine, and it was noisy. I looked up into that beautiful, night sky and had my first serious conversation with a holy God. I said, "God, I am nothing but a whore (*when you get under true conviction of The Holy Spirit, you start to call sin by the same words that God does*) and I will do anything if you will just somehow let me know you." I meant it with all my heart and He knew it.

God responded to me a day or two later. When I went to work, my first client, Cindy Leverette, walked into my beauty salon and said, "God told me to tell you how to be saved today."

I said, "Will it take long?" You see, I thought she would give me the official religious list of do's and don'ts and as I started to follow them, someday God would accept me.

Instead, she sat down, pulled out a small New Testament, looked at me and said, "Do you know you're a sinner?" She had no idea that I had just recently been convinced that I was probably the biggest sinner that ever lived.

I just said, "Yes."

She then showed me a picture of a man on one side of a great gulf and God on the other side with no way to bridge the gap. But the next picture showed the gap with a big cross connecting the two sides so that the man could walk across to God. She explained to me that because of my sin, I was separated from God with no hope. But then she went on to tell me that Jesus died on a cross and took my punishment and paid for every sin that I had ever committed or would ever commit. I could give Him my sin through confession, and He would give me His righteousness in return.

I was absolutely floored. I had never heard this in my life! Cindy then helped me pray a simple prayer confessing my sinfulness, and as I did, I felt God's love encompass me, and His presence filled my heart. The terrible weight of sin I had been carrying was gone. I was clean.

My Story: Part Two

"Surrender"

Now that I was clean, my eyes had been opened to God. I had a small glimpse of who He was, and I became what the Bible calls "a newborn babe, craving pure spiritual milk" (1 Peter 2:2). God's new life in me hungered for Him, and I did not even know that was supposed to happen or how it was supposed to happen. I told the man I was dating that I wanted him to take me to church, and he did. From the outside looking in, no one would have thought the God of the universe was at work in my circumstances, but He was.

I went to a little church in Jeremiah, Kentucky; the pastor's name was Bill Jones. I hung on every word, tears brimming in my eyes the whole time. I went back that Sunday night, and when he gave the altar call, I came out of the pew like a charging bull. I wanted all of God that I could get. I prayed with Pastor Jones that night at that altar, and he told me that I needed to get baptized.

I could not get enough of church. Pastor Jones was an expository preacher, which means that he would start in a certain book of the Bible and teach it verse by verse. Keep in mind that I knew ***nothing*** about the Bible and what it had to say about ***anything***, so I soaked it up like a sponge. One Sunday, as I sat there beside this man who was not my husband, Pastor Jones began his sermon, picking up where he had left off the last time. He started reading from I Corinthians 7:10-12. It says, "To the married I give this command (not I, but the Lord): A wife must not separate from her husband, but if she does, she must remain unmarried or else be reconciled to her husband. And a husband must not divorce his wife."

Well, what a shocker! When I left Rick, everyone told me that the God they served would want me to be happy. Not one person in my life told me what the Bible said. They all told me exactly what would make me feel better. I learned a valuable lesson from that, and it's this: Don't ask for my advice unless you want to hear the truth. I do not have many personal opinions. What I know is "thus says the Lord," and I trust what He says over any opinion I could ever have.

I started praying about what God would have me to do because I really did not want to go back to Rick. However, I had an unrest about being with the man I was dating (that, of course, was the Holy Spirit working in me), and I told God that I would leave him if that was His will. I also told Him that I would go to Africa and be a missionary or anything else He had in mind—anything except going back to Rick. In fact, I decided that I didn't want to be married at all. I would just live for God. I thought since He had gone to the trouble of saving someone so hip and cool and cute (meaning me, of course), then He must really have some big plans for my future. Given the lifestyle I had been living, I obviously didn't know many Christians, but I thought the ones I did know were a bunch of sticks in the mud, and I was going to be the energetic force they needed. I know, I know—that line of thinking was absolutely foolish, but I told you I was going to be honest, and that's how I honestly felt.

I gave God many choices of what I thought He and I could do together, and I was waiting for an answer. I was willing to allow God to pick anything other than my going back to Rick and I would be on it with my whole heart. No answer. I didn't realize God doesn't make deals like that.

My discomfort in my situation was increasing by the day, and God was even starting to give me the desire for Rick again. I started to miss him. Back then, I wasn't yet familiar with the Scripture passage in Philippians 2:13, which states, "For it is God who works in you to will and to act according to His good purpose." So He was working in my heart and spirit as I prayed. He was changing my desires into His desires as I sought His will. That is what prayer does.

One Wednesday night in church, I had the overwhelming urge to call Rick and ask him if I could come back to him. I wrote a note to the girl I had been staying with (she was sitting with me in the church service) telling her what I wanted to do. She just looked at me in surprise. After church we went to her apartment, and I called Rick. No answer. I called his boss (someone I had never called before or since) and asked if he knew where Rick was. He said my name out loud and then told me that he didn't know where he was but might see him later. I asked him to have Rick call me and gave him the number where I could be reached (remember, this was before everyone had cell phones).

Denise, the girl I was staying with, wanted to take me to talk to the preacher because she wasn't so sure about what I was doing. We called, and he said we could come on over. When we sat down, I started telling him my story. I also let him know that I could tell he had been basing his sermons on me and my situation. I guess I still thought I was the center of the universe; old habits die hard. To my surprise, he said, "Until this moment, I never knew you were married, but the Holy Spirit did."

Wow! God was proving Himself to be pretty awesome to me. Bill talked to me, and as I told him how I was feeling, he told me that I reminded him of the woman at the well. I thought to myself, "Hmmm, a Biblical woman." Those of you who know the Bible can chuckle, but at the time, I didn't realize who she was. Bill hit the nail on the head, and if you doubt it, read the story for yourself in the fourth chapter of John. Bill told me that I was doing the right thing, and God would bless me for it. He prayed with me, and I was beginning to be filled with incredible Holy Spirit joy as I went through that night. I didn't understand what was happening, but I now understand that as you operate in the will of God, He fills you with Himself and bears witness that you are doing the right thing.

I got back to Denise's and called Rick again. When he answered, he was very curt, but I pressed on and said, "I want to come home if you'll forgive me."

He said, "I'll forgive anything—just come home."

Looking back now, I can see how God's hand had orchestrated everything about that night—the feelings I had during the church service, the conversation with the pastor, not being able to talk to Rick before I talked to the pastor, even my means of transportation to get back to Rick—the man I had been dating had taken my car to have it cleaned that day, which meant that I did not have to go to his house to get the car. That way, I didn't have to face him. I got in my car with only the clothes on my back and raced to Johnson City, Tennessee where Rick and I had lived before I left him. Remember, we had moved back and forth because I was not happy and, I had concluded that it was Rick's fault that I was so miserable. But that night, as I thought about it, I realized that even after leaving Rick and finding someone else, I was still unhappy. After all this time, I finally understood that I was always taking the problem with me every time I moved, whether I was changing locations or men. The problem was me! Today, I realize that it is a good thing that Jesus became "my man," and His presence is where I live. Without Him, I would probably still be running from place to place.

I was so full of the joy of the Lord that it was overwhelming to me. I figured it might be overwhelming for Rick, too; I wouldn't have been surprised to discover that my face was shining just like the face of Moses after he'd spent time in the Lord's presence!

As we sat in The Waffle House the next morning, Rick shared with me that he had been sitting on the couch next to his boss when I had called the first time. He had motioned that he did not want to talk to me because he didn't want to be emotional in front of all the guys he was watching football with. After my call to his boss, he had headed home, which put him on the road home at the same time that I was talking to the preacher. And when the preacher and I finished our talk, I got to Denise's just in time for us to make contact by phone. Whew! Talk about timing! How does God do all that and keep the whole world turning?

But if my face was shining with God's glory like Moses, then Moses and I had something else in common: Moses had to cover his face because God's glory started to fade as time passed, and the glory and bliss that I felt started to fade, too. I had no idea what a walk with God was supposed to be, so I thought that if I didn't have a warm, fuzzy feeling all the time, something must be wrong. I realized that Rick was the same person and that I still didn't think I wanted to be married. It just about killed me to hurt him again, but I did—and I have to tell you that it is still very painful to even write this down and to have to think about it now.

I told God that I had tried His way and it didn't make me happy, so now I wanted "Plan B." I left and did some things that I never should have. The problem I now faced was that I had known the power of God by being in His will, which made the misery I was feeling outside of that will worse than any I had felt before. I would wake up in the morning, and for the first time in my life, I really didn't want to live.

A few weeks after leaving Rick, I found out I was pregnant. I felt like Jonah in reverse: instead of being in a whale, I felt like I had a little whale inside of me. God used this circumstance to help me quit waffling back and forth with what I should do. I called Rick, and my sweet man was happy and wanted me back—again. He is so much like Jesus in his love for me. And more incredibly, he has never thrown any of this in my face, ever. He is my hero.

Since Rick and I were officially divorced, we had to officially remarry. I was attending church with my uncle who was a Christian, and I approached his pastor about remarrying us. He agreed that we were doing the right thing, so a date was set for the ceremony. It was close to Christmas, and the wedding party was the pastor, his wife, Rick, and me. The church was huge, and I felt very small, insignificant, and very much a big failure. I was quickly getting over my pride in thinking that God had saved somebody as hip and cool as me. As we walked into the church, I was stunned to find that it was completely decorated for a big wedding—somebody else's big wedding had taken place that day and all the decorations were still there. Because it was the Christmas season, there was an enormous poinsettia tree in addition to the beautiful wedding decorations. The pews were decorated, and the altar was ready and prepared for the ceremony. There was even a unity candle that the pastor let us light during our ceremony so we could show our only official witness in the sanctuary—the Holy Spirit—that we were truly "one." It was beautiful, but it means even more to me now than it did then because I now know much more about how God works. How sweet of God to put His stamp of approval on our rejoining, and to (figuratively speaking) throw us a party that we did not pay a dime for.

Mercifully, God let us move from Tennessee to North Carolina so I would not have to face everyone I knew and could have a fresh start. Instead of coming clean with Rick about all I had done while I was gone, I just covered up my sin and decided that since I had finally obeyed God, then God would just have to be satisfied with what I had given Him. I didn't fully surrender my life, but I thought I was doing more than most people since I actually went back to my husband.

As it turned out, there was another Scripture passage that I didn't know was in the Bible: "He who conceals his sins does not prosper, but whoever confesses and renounces them finds mercy" (Proverbs 28:13). God is painfully true to His Word. I wasn't prospering. I'm not talking about money; I'm talking about spiritual prosperity. I felt so guilty about my life that I didn't want to talk to God about it. When I would try to read the Bible, condemnation would flood over me. So I did what most unsurrendered Christians do; I stayed in church and decided I would be the best Christian in the world from that point on. I would do my best to never disappoint God again. I only listened to Christian radio, went to church every time the doors were open, and made sure my children and husband obeyed every rule I felt God approved of (and there were many).

I felt like I was carrying the weight of the world on my shoulders and if anybody sinned against God, it was my fault for not making sure they were behaving. The Bible says the letter (of the law) kills, but the Spirit gives life. Keeping all those rules took all my joy and I was miserable. I could fake it most of the time (like in the old days). But I also found I just couldn't enjoy sin anymore. I was ruined for both worlds—Christian and pagan.

I had three children within about five and a half years, and, of course, homeschooled them. I say "of course" because that's what we serious Christians do. We don't want the world to taint our children. I knew there was no joy in my Christian life, so I sure didn't want my children to experience sin because I knew how much fun that lifestyle could be. Today, I'm glad I homeschooled my children, but my reasons then and now are totally different. I'm just driving home what a legalist I was. You will never meet a more sincere person than a legalist; they are truly trying to do everything they know to do to please God. But

I know from personal experience how deadly this "works" mentality is to a Christian. It is just miserable. And inadvertently, you start to become everyone's judge. You size people up and figure out all their shortcomings without even meaning to. It's so much easier to look at others than to look at a Holy God and have to see yourself in His light.

I was very comfortably steeped in this lifestyle, respected in my church, loved in my family, and I thought that I would just have to live in my hypocrisy forever. I had very legitimate reasons for not getting right with God. I was looking out for my family. To get right with God would cost me and my children far too much. In the back of my mind, I would soothe my conscience by thinking I would finally surrender fully to God when my youngest child was eighteen. That way, it would not affect them all so much. This delay bought me time, since my youngest child was only a year old). Whew! To think of the damage that I would have done by now if I had maintained that way of living makes me shudder.

In 1996, I attended a revival meeting at my church, and Bill Stafford was our guest speaker. That man will never know the impact he has had on my life. As I watched and listened to him preach, I could tell that he was one with God and the power, humor, love, sincerity, and fun that poured through him with such freedom was something we humans cannot fake. I was experiencing what is often referred to as "sitting under the Holy Spirit." The difference between the Holy Spirit's preaching and a man's preaching is like the difference between night and day. I sat there in awe of God and thought to myself, *(I don't know how that man got what he's got, but I would die to get it)*. I came home, and in my excitement, thought I had experienced revival. I started reading my Bible a little bit and came across a Scripture passage that I took as mine. It was from the book of Job, and it read, "Though He slay me, yet I will trust in Him" (Job 13:15).

I didn't realize it at the time, but repentance and revival are not something we drum up; they are gifts that God offers. Shortly after my "revival," I was invited to a Bible study called "What Happens When Women Pray." I looked forward to getting out a little and my testimony of remarriage was a quick way to approval in any Baptist crowd. I was going along nicely in this study when all of a sudden, I got to chapter three and the heading read, "If I regard iniquity in my heart, the Lord will not hear me" (Psalm 66:18 KJV). I read the chapter, and it was as if my whole body went limp and fear went into the marrow of my bones. This chapter talked about total surrender and nothing short, with all sins given to God, confessed to a person or persons or openly if need be. It was basically saying that if I wanted to live for God and know His presence and power, I would have to give Him one hundred percent of me. I truly felt God's Spirit letting me know that He was finished with my games, my playing church, and my fake, happy Christian face.

Oswald Chambers puts this better than I ever could in this January 15th devotional from his book, My Utmost for His Highest:

"Buried with Him . . . that . . . even so we
also should walk in newness of life."
Romans 6:4

"No one enters into the experience of entire sanctification without going through a "white funeral"—burial of the old life. If there has never been this crisis of death, sanctification is nothing more than a vision. There must be a "white funeral," a death that has only one resurrection—a resurrection into the life of Jesus Christ. Nothing can upset such a life; it is one with God for one purpose, to be a witness to Him.

Have you come to your last days really? You have come to them often in sentiment, but have you come to them really? You cannot go to your funeral in excitement, or die in excitement. Death means you stop being. Do you agree with God that you stop being the striving, earnest kind of Christian you have been? We skirt the cemetery and all the time refuse to go to death. It is not striving to go to death, it is dying, "Baptized into His death (Romans 6:3)."

Have you had your "white funeral," or are you sacredly playing the fool with your soul? Is there a place in your life marked as the last day, a place to which the memory goes back with a chastened and extraordinarily grateful remembrance, "Yes, it was then, at that 'white funeral,' that I made an agreement with God."

"This is the will of God, even your sanctification . . . ." (I Thess. 4:3). When you realize what the will of God is, you will

> *enter into sanctification as naturally as can be. Are you willing to go through the "white funeral" now? Do you agree with Him that this is your last day on earth? The moment of agreement depends upon you."* (Chambers, 1995)

These are some things I had to do to start the journey to my "white funeral." I made a list of all the sins that I had previously covered when I had told God He would just have to accept my partial surrender. I don't have the list anymore, but here are some of the major things on it.

(1) Stealing money from a place I worked as a teenager so I could go to a Van Halen concert. (For the record and for the sake of my mother who might read this someday, I was raised better than that. And for the sake of every other sinner who might read this someday, just remember that Adam and Eve had the perfect Parent, and they still sinned.)
(2) Using a permanent to curl someone's hair at a beauty shop where I worked and not paying for it.
(3) Cheating on my taxes as a business owner.
(4) Not telling my husband the truth about past things he could have divorced me for.
(5) Lying about something that was so embarrassing that I vowed to take it to my grave (God will never be my Lord if I don't do whatever He says, so He only let me take this to my "white funeral." Thank goodness, and now I'm free from it). I now share it freely and openly whenever I feel God wants me to.

I went to a church service during this time, and the preacher was talking about being sure of your salvation. He invited people to come to the front and "get it settled." I had tried that before and just went home more miserable. I wondered if you could ever really be sure. Was I one of those people who blasphemed the Holy Ghost—the "unforgivable sin" I'd read about? Why would God not answer me? I was getting mad at Him. I thought (*Do You just dangle salvation and the assurance of Your presence out in front of us, and then play 'catch-Me-if-you-can?'*).

I got up the next morning and read my Bible, which I was finally reading every day. I was reading straight through and was in the Book of Joshua. This is what I read in my anger and desperation:

> "The Lord said to Joshua, 'Stand up!' What are you doing down on your face? Israel (*Yes, it read "Israel" but it might as well have read "Terri")* has sinned; they have violated My covenant, which I commanded them to keep. They have taken some of the devoted things, they have stolen, they have lied, they have put them with their own possessions. That is why the Israelites cannot stand against their enemies; they turn their backs and run because they have been made liable to destruction. I will not be with you anymore unless you destroy whatever among you is devoted to destruction" (Joshua 7:10-12).

I shut my Bible and went for a walk. I still did not get it. You see, God reveals His Word to you by His Spirit when He speaks to you. You can study the Bible intellectually and learn many things, but it's different when you know that God has spoken. He truly has to open our minds to receive what He is revealing. As I was walking through the neighborhood, all of a sudden, God opened my mind, and I knew that Scripture was for me. That was the first time I ever experienced that kind of revelation. He used that Scripture and let me know that my fear and lack of victory was because of all the sin that I had committed and was keeping hidden. He was also gravely warning me that I had better come clean.

I remembered the victory I experienced when I obeyed God and came back to Rick, seven years earlier. I had thought that God would just do things in my life on my terms and be happy for what He could get. I was wrong.

I'm so glad that God is awesome and a consuming fire. I am so glad that He did not leave a single stone in my life unturned. Anything I would have kept to myself would have meant spiritual death for me. Unless you lose your life, you will never find it (Matthew 10:39).

I came home and literally wanted to fall on my face in awe of Him. He had finally spoken to me! After all that silence and fear, to hear anything was the greatest relief of my life, and it got me started down a road of obedience—true and total obedience. I wrote the IRS and confessed my tax problem, sent money to the place where I had worked as a teenager, paid back money for the permanent kit—all with letters of apology and without excuses, taking full responsibility for my sin. I started to see over again what an offense I was to God, not because of my sin this time, but my self-righteousness. Trying to behave well enough for God to accept me—what an affront to a Holy God! Jesus died for all of that, so how dare I try to appease Him any other way?

I talked to a friend of mine and asked her if she would homeschool my kids if I went to prison because of the tax problem, and she assured me she would. I told God that I would rather be free and sitting in prison than be in this prison in my heart. At least I would know that there was no sin hindering me from being able to pray for my children.

As I was going through this time, I was so afraid that I thought I might have a mental breakdown. What spurred me on to want to grab hold of God and be a display of His power was my babies. When I thought about going through life with my dead religion that I was feeding them, I realized one day they would move past "Jesus Loves Me" songs and see that my faith was dead. Kids will believe anything when they are little, but kids are smart when it comes to our talk vs. walk. I had a mental picture of me standing before Jesus on Judgment Day—a born again believer but without Jesus' power and having to watch my three children going to hell because of my hypocrisy. In my vision, I looked back to His face, and He said, "What was worth holding onto so hard that it cost you this?" I vowed that nothing would stop me from going all the way with God.

I had mailed my letters, and now I had to face my precious husband—the man who had suffered so much pain over the years because of me. The night before I was going to tell Rick everything, I lay in bed tossing and turning and picturing his face. And if that were not enough to worry about, I also was thinking of calling everyone (my pastor included) and telling them all about a big lie in my life. My only solace was thinking that at least I didn't have to get up tomorrow and be stretched out on a cross, naked, like Jesus was. He had to bear shame that He didn't deserve. I deserved mine.

I found myself saying to Him, "God, You're killing me!"

And I felt Him whisper to my soul, "Though He slay me, yet I will hope in Him" (Job 13:15). Now I knew why He had given me that Scripture when I thought I had experienced revival. He wanted me to go to my own funeral. Notice He didn't tell me that everything was going to be okay. He just let me know that I was to hope in Him, not anyone else. The only other thing I could think to say was, "Thy will be done." Little did I know that those were my magic words. I meant them with all my heart, even if it meant death to my reputation (again), my marriage, my children (by my absence if I went to prison), and my freedom.

I went to sleep and when I got up, I went trembling to Rick. I started confessing—but after only a little while, he stopped me and with so much kindness told me that it was all in the past and that I never had to come tell him anything again. I was forgiven. God knew he was going to do that and I spent all those years in fear for nothing.

Then I called my Bible study teacher and told her that I was going to call everyone and tell them my big lie. I was surprised when she told me that I did not have to do that—I just had to refuse to tell the lie again.

I said, "Theresa, is this you or God talking, because I'm getting to God!"

She told me of something similar in her life and how God showed her that she did not have to "fix" it all, just not to lie about it anymore. I hung up the phone and knew I had completed all that God showed me to do. I expected nothing more than a clear conscience, but I got much, much more. Sometime later, during the ordinary activities of that day, God came to me in a way that I will never forget. There is a Scripture passage in Exodus that parallels what happened to me:

". . . And Moses finished the work. Then the cloud covered the Tent of Meeting, and the glory of the Lord filled the tabernacle. Moses could not enter the Tent of Meeting because the cloud had settled upon it, and the glory of the Lord filled the Tabernacle" (Exodus 40:33b-34).

I can't explain it, but God did that same thing in my soul and I could barely sleep for almost three days. His glory was resting on me in a way I cannot describe. At one point, during those three days, as I walked in my neighborhood, I held up my hand and told God that He was going to have to stay His hand or I might die of sheer joy. He had filled me with His presence and (to borrow a phrase from Beth Moore), "There ain't no high like the Most High!" That was about seventeen years ago, and I am more excited about God now than I have ever been. He has transformed my whole life from glory to glory. How I praise his wonderful Name!

As an endnote, I want to let all readers know that my sin was never the problem. My sin was taken care of on the cross. It was my self-will and lack of surrender that made it impossible for me to walk with Christ. "Can two walk together unless they be agreed?" (Amos 3:3 KJV). At any time during all of my sin clean-up that I had truly gotten to the "Thy will be done" part, I could have had freedom. I was, perhaps, just a little more stiff-necked than most.

The Editing Story

Since I'm not a writer by profession, I obviously don't have an editor on my speed dial, but God does. I've found through the years that if He calls you to a task, He will equip you with what you need. When I got what I felt was confirmation God wanted me to write this book, I rested in the fact that He knew what He was doing and that He also knew I could barely operate WordPerfect (yes, my computer is that old) on my Dell. As I said in the previous chapter, I felt like He wanted this book to be in my own words, but I knew He wouldn't want it in my "own punctuation." I was wracking my brain trying to think of someone who would edit for me on my budget, which was faith. I thought maybe I could find someone who would be willing to edit first and get paid later, assuming the book would get published. I'm sometimes not sure if I have a great amount of faith or a great amount of naiveté. At any rate, if I feel I have heard from God, I am hard to stop.

In the middle of my thought process, I had to walk to a neighbor's house for some reason. On my way, I ran into a neighbor, who is a great friend of mine, who happened to be out in her yard with her granddaughter. Her name is Jane. She is one of my entire family's favorite people. My older son loves her so much because he says she is a smart-alecky Christian. That may not sound like a compliment to some, but it is the highest compliment from my Andrew. He can't stand cookie-cutter Christians that always seem to get in line with marching orders like a politician, always giving the right answer whether he or she believes it or not. Jane makes you think and challenges you when necessary, and she doesn't mind or take it personally when we "agree to disagree."

I never hear Jane complain, and she is always ready with a listening ear (not to mention a hot cup of coffee or a cold glass of lemonade). You would think by being around her that she didn't have a care in the world. Of course, we all know that no one lives in a care-free world, and that is especially true of Jane. The past few years of her life have been spent caring for her elderly mother who was slowly dying from Alzheimer's. In the final weeks of her mother's life, my friends Vickie Vaughan and Brenda Hill, my mother Sue, and I assisted Jane and her sister in taking care of their mother on those days when the Hospice workers weren't scheduled to come. Anyone who has taken care of an elderly, sick person knows that it is often dirty and unpleasant work that can stretch on for hours. It humbled me to watch Jane. She was so tender, patient, and kind. She reminded me of a mother, watching over one of her little ones who was sick.

I don't think anyone can fully understand the stress of being a full-time caregiver until they have actually been one. I guess it's an exclusive club that not many people line up to join. Her mother was bed-ridden, so it was a very physical job. That may not sound like a big deal until you understand that Jane nearly lost her life years ago. She was in her front yard, getting ready to cross the street to attend a Sunday morning church service, when an out-of-control truck came screaming around a curve and hit her, throwing her thirty-five feet through the air. Within the next thirty-six hours, she underwent two major operations to repair the broken bones in her right leg and her back.

The damage done to her body was enormous, but the healing it brought to her soul was something only Jesus could do. God had her undivided attention and He used the healing time to slow her down and reveal Himself to her. Unbelievably, she says it's the best thing that ever happened to her. As I see her going about "doing good" (like taking home cooked meals to people who are in some kind of need and baking goodies at Christmastime for everyone on our street), I think of Jacob. Since her accident, Jane walks with a limp, but like Jacob, she walks with God. She's a hero of mine.

Now, back to my walk to the other neighbor's house—as Jane and I were talking and catching up, I mentioned to her that I was writing a book. The next words out of her mouth were, "Terri, I do editing for people." Actually, Jane sent me an email after our visit in her yard, which I kept because as soon as I got it, I knew it had to be one of my stories. You can read her own words for yourself as I've copied and pasted the email she sent to me the evening after our talk.

> *"The funny thing is that when I opened my mouth, I had no idea that 'Terri, I do editing for people' was what I was going to say. It popped into my brain and fell out of my mouth. You know that I've been waiting ever since Mother died for God to give me my next assignment. I had no idea what it would be, but He's had me more or less sitting on the shelf for quite some time, and I was honestly beginning to wonder what the hold-up was. He's allowed me to rejoin my church's choir and Cantamos (*another choir that she belongs to*), and He's given me a wonderful opportunity at my church to begin a program that involves the laity in presenting different parts of the worship service, and I'm grateful for that. But I've also definitely felt 'resistance' from Him on other things I've considered doing. Last night, I told Him that I was afraid that I'm getting lazy and indifferent and boring. Guess that wasn't what He had in mind.*
>
> *This is going to be fun.*
>
> *Jane* <><

I don't understand how editing is fun but I'll take her word for it. The beautiful part about Jane editing for me is that she knows me and loves me. She gets my humor and knows my heart. It's so amazing to watch her take my stories (that can have some abominable sentence structure) and make them flow beautifully, but still sound exactly like me. The words from Ephesians 3:20 are so true, "Now to Him who is able to do immeasurably more than all we ask or imagine . . . ."

And sometimes He does it during a simple walk down the street.

Writing the IRS Story

I decided to include this anti-climactic story in this book because after I speak, so many people want to know what happened after I wrote the IRS. As usual, God takes the ordinary stuff of life and teaches extraordinary lessons if only we will tune in and listen.

As you read earlier in "My Story," you saw that God had me clean out this temple called "Terri Broome" so that He could fill me with His Spirit, and part of that cleaning involved dealing with the IRS. My fear of God making me come clean about my unpaid taxes made me not want to get too specific with Him with regard to all that internal housekeeping in what nominal prayer life I had. I just prayed generic prayers if I prayed at all. When I would go to God, I felt like David when he said in Psalm 32:3, "When I kept silent, my bones wasted away . . . ." Unconfessed sin takes away your very energy and zest for life. Unfortunately, we can live an entire life like this. What I found was that days turned into weeks, weeks turned into months, and months turned into years, and God's voice got fainter and fainter. Then it became normal to not hear from God. I remember hearing Bill Stafford say, "If you haven't heard from God in two weeks, you're backslid!" I know that's poor grammar, but it's a mighty big truth. I thought he was kind of crazy the first time I heard him say that since I hadn't heard from God in about seven years. Funny how we judge truth by our own experiences. Now, when I hear someone make a statement that I disagree with, I try to search scripture and see if I'm the one who's wrong instead of always thinking I'm right when I differ with someone.

When I went to that little Bible study that changed my life years ago, the scripture that arrested my soul was, "If I regard iniquity in my heart, the Lord will not hear me" Psalm 66:18. I realized that I was playing games with God, I wasn't going to fool Him, and I certainly wasn't going to win. Losing with God could mean losing the souls of my children. If the stakes had not been so high, I'm sure I would still be playing those games. I could talk all day long about God to my children and make sure they were 'good', but God didn't have access to them through my spirit. I was just putting rules on them and they were obeying beautifully. I was teaching them to be like me, good little hypocrites. I judged all the children that weren't as good as mine and swelled with pride as I would discuss everyone else's shortcomings. Today I love misbehaving children just like I love well-behaved children. I love because I have the love of God in me. Oh, how dangerous hypocrisy is because it blinds us to who we really are and definitely to who God really is! Because we were all well-behaved on the outside, I thought God must be really impressed with us. I was setting my kids up to be so good that they wouldn't need the Holy Spirit's help, just like I was living. We lead our kids in the paths that we think we've covered. Jesus said, "Blessed are the pure in heart," and I was teaching my kids, "Blessed are those that control themselves constantly and never mess up." I was setting up my precious children for a terrible future.

As I write this, my heart overflows with thankfulness that I now understand what lives in us all (our sinful nature), and my children know that I don't expect anything from them apart from Christ. They have now been taught that in them (their sinful nature) dwells no good thing. They know that Christ in them is their only hope and that I wouldn't be shocked or surprised at anything they could ever come to me with. They would receive mercy and love. They don't wear my ego on their shoulders. They are free to fail. If and when they sin (and they do, and they will), I don't panic; I just pray that their sin will lead them to Christ and that they will long to be free like they were created to be.

As I was contemplating writing the IRS, I asked my best buddy, Glenda Mitchell, if she would homeschool my kids if I went to prison, and she said that she would. I was convinced that my only ministry was going to be a prison ministry soon, and I was trying to emotionally prepare to leave my babies. The only thing that comforted me was that

I would no longer be in prison in my spirit and soul (the worst kind of prison); it would only be my body that was imprisoned. My spirit would be free to talk to the Living God, and prison walls couldn't stop that. I could pray for my children even though I wouldn't be physically with them. That became more important to me than anything. Funny how when we start to obey God, we think He will allow the absolute worst thing imaginable to happen to us. We think He is so hard and mean. That's because until He floods us with His Spirit from outside of us, our only point of reference is ourselves. We think He is mean and vindictive like us. Oswald Chambers said, "We think God is mean because we are."

I was in that little Bible study and we were covering the scripture in James that said to confess your faults (sins) to each other so that you may be healed. I didn't have the courage to talk about my tax evasion yet, so I confessed a lesser sin to the person I was paired up with. I was still desperately trying to cling to my dignity. I had stolen some money as a teenager from where I worked to go to a Van Halen concert. I wrote the owner of the theatre and confessed, paying back more than I remembered taking. The person I had been paired up with said that she thought that was wonderful and proceeded to say, "My Sunday School teacher had to write the IRS and confess cheating on his taxes!" Talk about a heavenly brick on the head! I was cornered and told her that I did that, too. Coupling that confirmation with a conversation I heard on the radio with Kay Arthur and then Larry Burkett saying basically the same thing about cheating the government, I knew God was serious and I better get serious, too. Fear was just so paralyzing.

I wrote the letter to the IRS and asked my friend Glenda to pray with me for a name and address to send it to. I was secretly hoping that God wouldn't be able to provide something so specific and hoping that writing the letter would be enough. Oh how funny that thought is to me now! He could create human beings, shut the mouths of lions, part the Red Sea, but surely He didn't have the address for Uncle Sam or know anyone's name that worked there. As I was going through some old records from a business we owned, I came across a letter from the IRS, and on it was a name and address for 'The Problem Resolution Office.' Whew! My fear of Uncle Sam disappeared under the shadow of the Almighty. I was realizing that God knew ***everything***. That may seem like a no-brainer, but when you experience His power like that, it is very humbling and awe-inspiring.

I took my letter I had written and put that name and address on it. I made no excuses for my dishonesty. I said I was a cheat and liar and quoted something from Deuteronomy. When I think of all that now, I can just see that lady opening my letter in her cubicle and saying to her neighbors, "Come here, guys, and get a load of this nut case!" As I have often said, I was either going to the nuthouse or to my Father's house, but I wasn't staying where I was. If I wouldn't have obeyed God and gotten the power of the Holy Spirit, I fear that I would be crazy by now and I'm not kidding. We were created to be filled with God's Spirit, and a lack of God in a human being is a dangerous thing. We were created to be consumed . . . by God. If we are not consumed by Him, we will be consumed by something. He is the only thing that can consume us and not destroy us. Being consumed by Him brings us glorious life.

The day I was headed to the post office, a young friend stopped by the house. She was a very sweet girl I had been trying to talk into becoming a Christian for a couple of years. During my time of brokenness, God showed me I just needed to hush and quit telling people about Him and how wonderful it was to know Him since I was lying. I didn't have a robust relationship with God, and He let me know that He didn't need me to help Him get His will done down here. He wanted me to stop all my foolishness and get serious about talking **to** Him instead of always talking **about** Him. I asked my friend if she wanted to ride to the grocery store and post office with me since she had pulled up as I was getting ready to leave. She agreed to go. I started to tell her about my deadness and how I was getting serious with God. She went with me to the post office and since I had my babies with me and was carrying them, she filled out my certified letter to the IRS.

She came back home with me and couldn't get enough of my honesty. I didn't pretend to have all the answers anymore; I just told her the raw truth about myself. She told me that it was scaring her. I let her know that it was scary to think of meeting God. She said that she wanted to ask Him into her life. We went into the bedroom and got on our knees. She humbly asked Christ to forgive her and save her soul. That was seventeen years ago, and last time we talked, she was faithfully following Him.

A few weeks later, I heard back from the IRS. They told me what I sent them was past the statute of limitations. Some of it was, but a small portion of unreported income from teaching an exercise class wasn't. I was distraught. I was so serious about being clean and right before God that I vowed to "make them make me pay!" I thought my sin was the problem, but I was wrong. God doesn't allow us to fear anything or anyone and walk with Him. This was my road of humility, and because I was so proud and stiff, I actually had to go this far for a clear conscience. I had obeyed God and that was all that mattered to Him. I thought I had to make every wrong I had ever done right. I would still be doing that if that was the case. He taught me a valuable lesson through this. He's so smart.

I was coming home from Bible study one day, and I ran a stop sign. The police stopped me and let me know I was guilty of running the stop sign. I agreed, of course, and to my surprise, she let me go without a ticket. I was so grateful and as I drove off; I felt like God whispered gently to me, "You're guilty, aren't you going to go and 'make them make you pay'?" Of course that was a rhetorical question and was used to drive home a point. They knew I was guilty, but they let me go free. The IRS knew I was guilty, and they let me go free. He was letting me know that I was free. Early on in my surrender, as you see from my stories, I didn't know God's nature very well. He graciously has shown me over and over that He cares about my heart and my willingness to be pliable in His precious hands . . . like a potter and clay. He doesn't expect me to be perfect; He wants me totally surrendered to Him so He can pour His wonderful perfection through this jar of clay.

The Dream Story

After true surrender of my will to God's will, my life became dramatically different on the inside, but nothing really changed outwardly. I was still staying home with my kids, schooling them each day, doing housework, and so forth. I found surrender didn't give me a better life at all outwardly. What it did give me was eyes to see.

Hebrews 4:13 says that, "Nothing in all creation is hidden from God's sight. Everything is uncovered and laid bare before the eyes of Him to whom we must give account." I started to see that God had always known what lurked deep in my heart even though I didn't. What I now knew He saw was that I was a manipulator, self-centered, had self-serving motives; in short: self, self, self. I was full of it. Now that I was full of the Holy Spirit, aka "The Spirit of Truth," He started to show me the truth about myself. Before being filled with the Spirit, I was blind to all of this. I honestly thought I was very selfless, and I always loved it when everyone noticed how selfless I was. I thought I was wonderful because I did so much for others; of course, I always tried to never do things without an audience. I thought Rick didn't know how lucky he was to have me. Need I go on?

This is funny now, but I really lived in that place (sometimes called "my own little world") and have found through the years that many people live in their own little world, and they don't even know it. Jesus spoke of us church-goers as having "eyes that can't see and ears that can't hear, topped off with a hard heart." We listen all the time but it never sinks in. Truth goes in our ears, shines in our eyes, but then pings off of our hard hearts, which means that it can't go in and transform us. That's why we're warned over and over again in Scripture, "Today if you hear His voice, do not harden your heart" (Hebrews 3:15a). I fear a hard heart more than death, because a hard heart means spiritual death, and my spiritual life is what makes all the other aspects of my life—physical, emotional, and mental—worth living.

In my now tattered Bible, beside Revelation Chapter Three, written in green marker is a single word and a date. It says "Dream, 12-16-97." I was just getting my ears tuned to His voice and my eyes used to the brightness of His glorious Word, but I was having an issue trying to keep a soft heart. Since I had a real experience with the Living God, the Holy Spirit started to pour through me, and people started to be attracted to Him. I gave my testimony at my church and expected to be rejected as I just told the truth about myself, but instead, as I finished speaking and turned to leave the stage, I looked up and saw everyone standing and clapping, many with tears streaming. I didn't realize how much power He has when He has someone that doesn't hinder Him. Acts 1:8 says, "you ***will*** receive power when the Holy Spirit comes upon you." It's very humbling because you know it's not you; it's Him. Talk about mixed emotions—I found myself wanting to hit the floor and crawl under the carpet in humility but wanting to jump up and down with joy all at the same time. What Watchman Nee said about the Holy Spirit is very true, which is that you get ministered to as you let the Spirit flow through you. The people listening get blessed, but you also get blessed because He is pouring through your Spirit as He uses you to reach others. Oh, the joy of knowing God! It is unspeakable!

Women started calling me all the time to talk about God, themselves, and their problems, and they seemed to believe I had all the answers. I had experienced God in such a way I started to think that I might have all the answers, too. Can't you just see the beautiful disaster starting to brew? I would get up in the morning to meet with God and the phone would start to ring. Well, of course I had to answer it because these people needed me. Although God was the One they needed, I wasn't sure He could get His will done without me. My youngest child wasn't even potty trained yet, and I was trying to save the world. My kids needed me all the time, but I had to do God's work, and it was wearing me out. I came to dread hearing the phone ring, but I had to answer it and sound all godly because that was expected. Without realizing it, I was doing something that was so dangerous: I was becoming a hypocrite in Jesus' Name. I had to act like I cared because I was holding up God's glory. I had to act like I loved because that was what people expected.

God let me go on like this until I couldn't take anymore. I had been surrendered to God for about a year but already the "cares of this world were choking out the Word" (Mark 4:19 KJV). Sometimes, the work we do in God's Name becomes the enemy because we're working hard **for** Him, not enjoying a love relationship **with** Him. Oh my goodness, the difference in the two is enormous!

As all of this pressure was building in me, I told Rick one afternoon I needed to go for a walk. With three young children, women calling all the time, plus the weight of the whole world on my shoulders, I felt like I had to get alone and talk to God. I wasn't sure how I got from great joy to the mess I was in, but I knew God had the answer and I was going to find it. I went for that walk and poured my heart out to God. I told Him I just couldn't keep doing what I was doing—at least, not the way I was doing it. I told Him I didn't have any extra love to give, and I was tired of people, but if this was what He called me to, I would do it. He would just have to turn up the "love machine" for me, because I was bone dry. I didn't get an answer right then, but I was trusting God heard my cry and would answer me. And boy, did He!

This is where the dream of this story's title comes in. I went to bed that night and quickly fell asleep. Sometime during the night, I started to dream. In my dream, I was in church, and I didn't have my children with me. After the service, I heard there was going to be another service. I didn't want to stay, but I was worried what all the church people would think if I left. All that mattered was what they thought of me, not where my children were or even the fact that I didn't want to be there. During the second service, we all started to go to sleep. We started to get very sleepy and started to lean to one side and I heard a voice say, "***Wake up***!" I woke up (in the dream, not in actuality) but quickly started to go to sleep again. The voice came a second time, "***Wake up***!" I suddenly snapped to (still dreaming, not in actuality) and thought to myself, "Where are my children?"

I ran out of church and got in the car. I raced home and saw my nephew and my middle son, Scott, walking through the back yard.

I screamed, "Where is Andrew?" and they shrugged their shoulders because they didn't know. Somehow I could see him in my mind waiting for me at school, all alone and afraid, and it was getting dark. The terror that shot through me in the dream literally woke me up. My heart was pounding, and I couldn't calm down or go back to sleep. I slipped out of bed and went to the living room and got my Bible. I started reading where I left off the day before, trying to figure out what the dream meant and if God was trying to tell me something. I think I was in Corinthians and was getting nothing from the text. I stopped reading and put my head back and asked God if He wanted me to read something else. Out of nowhere, I heard the words "Revelation Three" in my mind. I thought to myself, "Revelation? Scary!" With trembling hands, I turned there.

This is what I read in Revelation 3:1-3: "To the angel at the church in Sardis, write: These are the words of Him who holds the seven spirits of God and the seven stars. I know your deeds; you have a reputation for being alive but you are dead. ***Wake up***! Strengthen what remains and is about to die, for I have not found your deeds complete in the sight of my God. Remember, therefore, what you have received and heard; obey it, and repent. But if you do not ***wake up***, I will come like a thief, and you will not know at what time I will come to you."

As I read, I realized everything truly is open and laid bare before God. I was beginning to have a reputation as a person very connected to God, and I wasn't about to let anyone know that I felt very unplugged. But there was no way I could prevent God from knowing that, or anything else for that matter.

I had never had anything like that happen. It was Truth—God's Truth—held up right in my face. I found out God doesn't play games. He straight up tells you the truth. God knew exactly what was wrong with me even though I didn't. When I read the words "***Wake up***" twice, just like in my dream, I felt like my bone marrow melted. I was scared because I realized that I wasn't just reading about the church in Sardis—I was reading about myself! When I read that I had a reputation of being alive, but God knew I was dead inside, I felt so ashamed. I had lost connection with the only true source of power—Him. The great thing about God is that He not only shows you the problem, He gives you the answer to correct the problem. He doesn't heap guilt upon you; He leads you in truth. He showed me how to respond to this blinding truth. He showed me that I needed to repent.

What was I to repent of? The answer was church work and neglecting my home and children. He let me know that I was holding up a reputation, and He gave me the true definition of the word "reputation"—it is what people think, not what God knows. He wanted me to take care of my children because that was what He called me to as a young mother. He showed me how important my family was to Him and that what they thought about me was more important than what anyone else thought. He let me know failure with my children and husband would be complete failure to Him. My ministry was inside the four walls of my house. He wanted me to be Christlike there and to give my best to them, not everyone else. I was reminded of something Amy Carmichael said, "Children bind the feet of their mothers, and God meant for it to be that way."

I immediately let people know that I would no longer spend hours on the phone and that I would return calls when I could, because my family had priority. I praise God that He came in such a dramatic way and with nail-scarred hands; He ripped off the mask that I didn't even mean to put on. He loves us so much that He wounds us to heal us. Proverbs says, "Wounds from a friend can be trusted" (Proverbs 27:6). I'm glad for my Friend, and I do trust Him.

Surrender didn't make me any better—surrender gave me eyes to see and ears to hear Truth. It produced in me a soft heart that is able to respond instead of defend myself. Surrender gave me the ability to have true humility. The Bible says that God lives in a high and holy place but also in a contrite heart (Isaiah 57:15). The more I'm given over to God, the more I can be full of His Spirit. My flesh will never be any better, but it can be a conduit of the Living God. The reason I started to not like people and not truly care about them was because I was living by my flesh. I quickly found out that in this flesh dwells no good thing. Either I'm full of the Holy Spirit or full of self. I think this happens to so many people in ministry, and they never realize the problem. They start to minister out of their own flesh and it becomes a disaster. They become people-pleasers and people-haters. I think the two come as a pair. The root of being a people-pleaser is self-love. If you love God, you will reflect His Nature, but if you love self, you will reflect your sinful nature.

God is honest. He doesn't spare our feelings; He wields His Word like a surgeon's scalpel and cuts out our "self" cancers. Like cancer, we may not feel it, but it is growing and slowly destroying us. Jesus said in Luke 4:18, "He has sent Me to proclaim freedom for the prisoners and recovery of sight for the blind, to release the oppressed . . . ." That sums us all up: blind, captive, and oppressed. The only cure is the Holy Spirit. He opens our eyes, lets us out of prison, and banishes the oppression of self-interest. That is the meaning of "where the Spirit of the Lord is, there is freedom" (2 Corinthians 3:17). There is no greater freedom than being able to be full of God's Spirit, the ability to look Him in the face, agree with His verdict about everything, and then let Him set me free to let His Spirit flow—unhindered. That's living the dream!

Grandad's Story

Charles S. Jones, my stepdad and my children's "Grandad," was one of the most interesting and unique characters I have ever known. My parents divorced when I was eight, and after the strict upbringing I'd experienced with my biological dad, I didn't quite know what to think about this gregarious, drinking, cussing, big-hearted, and funny man that my mom eventually married. When I was about nine years old, we moved into an apartment across the street from Charlie. He started showing up to see if Mom needed anything done around the house; he obviously knew a cutie when he saw one.

I was the youngest of three children and probably the most easy-going, so I accepted Charlie much more readily than my older sister and brother. I had a very trusting and bubbly personality as a little child, and I naturally liked people, and they usually liked me. That was probably the reason I found myself being used as an excuse to get my mom and Charlie together. As an example, on one occasion, my mom's sister called Charlie because I had a bad earache and according to local folk medicine, smoke blown into your ear would cure an earache, and we needed his "smoky" help. Hey! Don't laugh! I grew up in southwestern Virginia where folk medicine was sometimes the only medicine practiced. My little brother got liquor in his baby bottle (mixed with Coca-Cola) to help his cough. I wish they had thought of that for my earache. It might not have cured it, but I'm sure I would have slept better.

Mom and Charlie got married, and when I was ten, they had a little boy named Scotty. He became my own little baby doll. I loved him so much that I almost felt like his second mommy. I have very fond memories of that time in my life. Charlie was rough around the edges, but having a family to care for and my mom to love softened him, and he became a very good stepdad to us and a good provider for the family. After I grew up and left home, I wrote him a letter to let him know that I appreciated the fact that he didn't make me feel like a stepdaughter. I felt that he loved me like his own.

When I became a Christian, Charlie was supportive, but I could tell that it caused a division between us. I no longer cussed, so I didn't like to hear cussing. I no longer drank and didn't approve of drinking. I guess you could say that I became a regular "church lady" and I'm sure he felt uncomfortable. I was getting my spiritual legs under me and thought it was my duty to be the judge of the world. Bless Charlie's heart for having to deal with all of that.

Thankfully, I didn't live in that legalistic world forever. God taught me about love and filled me with His love for Grandad. I tried to be a good example to him, but at times it was hard because although he could be so kind, he could also be really bad-tempered and would throw around words that my kids didn't hear anywhere but his house. I felt like I was walking a tightrope between honoring my parent and protecting my children—a tough position for a momma bear like me to be in!

When Charlie would come to visit us, I would invite him to church, but he never wanted to go. Also, when he was visiting, I wouldn't let him watch R-rated movies. When he got mad and asked "Why," I told him that it was because the Holy Spirit lived here. He didn't have a comeback for that. I hated to have to be that firm with him, but I decided that I was going to obey God no matter what it cost me.

I now fast forward to a time when I was visiting Mom and Grandad at their home. He was really hateful to her over something trivial, and I got mad. I guess you could say that I'm also a momma bear about anybody in my family, not just the cubs. After returning to my house, I called my sister Robin and told her what had happened. She got mad too. Right after that, Charlie happened to come by her house. He told her the same story I had, but his version made him sound innocent, and my mom sounded like the bad guy. Can anybody relate to that particular type of dysfunctional behavior? Robin looked at him and said, "That's not what Terri told me." When Charlie found out I had told her about it, he got mad—at me.

Charlie was a retired military man and wasn't used to anyone standing up to him like that and he was furious with me. Robin told me about it, and I thought that I had ruined our relationship. I had compassion for him, but at the same time, I hated the injustice of what he'd just done. I knew that he was wrong, and it seemed like he never took responsibility when he blew up, which was happening more and more often. Proverbs 29:22 says, "An angry man stirs up dissension, and a hot-tempered one commits many sins." I was angry with Charlie but also very worried because he was getting older, and I knew that he didn't know Christ. The road that he was on was leading to destruction, not only now but ultimately for eternity.

In the middle of this mess, I was desperate to get direction from God about how to handle what I was going through with Charlie. I always knew that God had a plan if I would just calm down and get before Him. As Beth Moore has said, "He is never wringing His Holy hands wondering what to do." My daily reading was Deuteronomy 3:29, and I felt that God wanted me to personalize what I read that morning. Here's what I wrote in my prayer journal: "Blessed are you, O Terri!" (It read "Israel" in my Bible, but I put my name there instead.) "Who is like you, a woman saved by the Lord? He is your shield and helper and your glorious sword. Your enemies will cower before you, and You will trample down their high places."

After I finished my quiet time with God that morning, Mom called and said that Grandad wanted to speak to me. I heard him in the background and could tell he was mad. I told her that it wasn't a good time because I was afraid of what I might say. Good time or not, Grandad got on the phone like a raging bull and let me have it. However as I listened, I felt God take hold of me and gave me total calm inside. In God's strength, I proceeded to "trample down all his high places." I let him know that his behavior was unacceptable to his family and to God. I told him that no one ever held him accountable for his bad temper, but that God saw it all and would ultimately hold him accountable for every word that came from his mouth. I also told him that I would never allow anyone to speak like he did in front of my children, including him. But I also assured him that he was my father figure and because of that, I was trying to honor him. I broke into tears and told him that when he used God's Name in vain, it made me feel scared for him and that I only wanted him to be in heaven with me some day.

By the end of that phone conversation, Charlie had changed from a raging bull to someone who was "cowering before me"—just as God's Word had assured me he would. God had been my shield, helper, and glorious sword.

I came out of my room and just collapsed into my husband's arms because it was so hard to have to say the things I said. I knew I had obeyed God by telling Charlie the truth, but I hated to hurt him. Sometimes honoring our parents means telling them truth that will hurt them in the short term, but will ultimately work for their good in the long term. My only goal for Grandad was to tell him the truth so that he would face what his life was without God and to make him think about where he would spend eternity. Everyone seemed to be afraid to confront Charlie, but the bottom line was that I loved him more than I loved being in his good graces. I thought that our relationship was over and that I would never be welcome in their house again. I was so upset about what happened, but my conscience was clear because I knew that my motives were pure. I felt that God wanted all that junk that I had kept bottled up all those years to be out in the open, for my good and for Grandad's.

My husband told me that I should write him a letter and tell him that I was concerned about his soul, so that's just what I did. As I was writing this story, I searched for that letter but I couldn't find it. As I remember it, I told him I feared he thought I considered myself better than him and that I was judging him, but the fact of the matter was that nothing could have been further from the truth. To put it simply, I explained that all of mankind was swimming in a sea of sin with no land in sight. Some are better swimmers than others, but eventually we are all going under. Jesus comes walking on the water toward each of us and extends His hand to rescue us from our helpless situation. I then said that the only difference between the two of us was that I had taken that hand. I told him that I used to hear his mother pray out loud for his soul. And I reminded him how much I loved him and appreciated him. I sent that letter out with both postage and prayer.

My sister went to visit our parents shortly after he received the letter and, as she was leaving, he followed her to the car and shared the letter with her. He sat and cried as she read it. When she told me that, I knew that God was softening that big old heart in preparation to make it His home.

Our relationship got so much better and more open after that time, but Charlie still didn't accept Christ. But I could tell that he was more interested in spiritual things. One night when I called just to chat with him and Mom, Charlie answered the phone. When I asked what he was doing, he told me that he had my letter out, reading it again. I told him over again how I meant every word and how much I loved him.

I'm not sure how much time went by, but while he and Mom were visiting my home one weekend, I got up early to read my Bible and pray. I was trying to be quiet, but Charlie woke up. I could tell that he wanted to talk, so I quit reading and just talked to him. He started to tell me about a movie that he had watched as a young man; it was a western movie, and all the characters in it either went to heaven or hell. He told me that it was scary. I talked to him about how I came to know Jesus, but in the midst of my story, Mom got up, so we quit talking about spiritual things. We had a good day, and they left for Virginia sometime that afternoon.

Around 7:00 that evening, Mom called and said that Grandad wanted to talk to me. She sounded so serious that I knew something was up. As I held the phone, Grandad was silent on the other end. I asked what was wrong, and I could tell that he wanted to talk, but tears were the only thing flowing freely on the other end of that line. I asked him if he was afraid of going to hell, and he choked out a very weak, "Yes." I asked him if he wanted to ask Jesus into his life and out came another weak "Yes." He was finally able to tell me that he had come all the way to North Carolina to get saved but had lost his nerve to talk to me about it. I led that sweet lamb in a simple prayer, and like a little child, he asked Jesus to save him from his sins. It was a precious time. After he prayed, he said that he wished his mommy (that's still what he called her at his age) was here to see what had happened to him.

So what was life like for Charlie after that? Well, he still cussed sometimes after he prayed that prayer, but he would look up and ask

God to forgive him. He doubted his salvation at times and felt like he ought to be a better Christian than he was. The Bible says that God lives in a high and holy place but also in a contrite heart. I looked up that "contrite," and it simply means "sorry for one's own sins." Grandad mourned over his life of sin, and being "sorry" for those sins definitely described him. Since he was in his seventies by the time he came to Christ, he found it was hard to be a spiritual baby at that age. He even told me that he was wondering what his life had meant up to that time. He felt like it had been a waste, and he had so many regrets. It made me sad for him.

Grandad got baptized at my church. When Pastor Ruffin talked to him about baptism, he was so emotional that his lips were quivering. Grandad was at the service when my older son Andrew played his guitar for Tataw, his other grandfather (another story in this book), and he heard Pastor Ruffin preach that day. He wanted Ruffin to know that his preaching had impacted him deeply and was a part of the reason that he was now saved. Ruffin was so gracious and kind to him that Grandad and I both got all weepy. When the baptism service began, Ruffin told a little about Grandad's salvation before he dunked him under the water. When he came up, the whole church broke into applause. Grandad, never a shrinking violet, turned toward the congregation, clasped his hands, raised them over his head, and celebrated unashamedly with everyone. After I returned to my seat, Andrew leaned over to me and said, "Grandad's working the crowd." We got hysterical. He **was** working the crowd! He loved to be the center of attention. Some things never change.

However, I saw Grandad's heart change and knew it was real. He couldn't stand to have an argument without apologizing, he loved to go to church, he never drank again (**big** miracle), and he was so hungry to understand the Bible. My sweet sister would go to visit and read it to him and then explain it. She lived closer to our parents than I did and she was like a lifeline to Grandad. They grew very close as she tried to help him in his walk with God. The last time she visited with him, she read from the fourth chapter of the book of Hebrews. She explained to Grandad that unbelief will keep us from fully experiencing what the Bible calls "God's rest." The Hebrews had been delivered (*their* salvation), but their unbelief kept them from the fullness and "rest" of that great salvation. Attaining that rest requires a mixing of faith with the Word. They had been saved, but they just weren't enjoying their salvation and resting in it—just like Grandad.

Not long after that reading Robin had with Grandad, he passed away. Privately, she asked God for assurance that Grandad was in heaven.

At the funeral service a few days later, without any knowledge of Robin and Grandad's last Scripture reading, the pastor stood up before the congregation and read the Scripture passage he had selected: the book of Hebrews, chapter four. It was a sure sign of God's assurance to Robin—indeed, to all of us—that Grandad, our sweet Charlie, was finally experiencing true "rest" in the presence of Christ.

The "Love" Story

Oh, how I love this story! When my stepdad passed away in 2008, I was asked to say a few words at the small service being held at the mausoleum. It was a beautiful spring day and my sister told me that Charlie had shared with her that he wanted to have his funeral on a day like this. So I started my talk with that little bit of information. I also told the people gathered there that when Robin, my sister, had asked me if I thought Charlie would approve of his obituary, I replied, "Yes, because it was the longest one in the section that day!" As I shared in the previous story, he was a big cut-up who loved to make people laugh, and I knew he would have appreciated the light-heartedness my little joke brought as so many of us were experiencing the pain of losing him.

I then went on to share the story of how Grandad was saved. The story made us all cry. After the service, a lady came up to me and said, "You don't know me, but . . . ."

When she touched my hand and I heard her voice, I said, "Your name is Love." Now I have to tell you that I didn't recognize her face at all, but I recognized Jesus in her.

By her reaction, I could tell that I was right. I proceeded to say, "I met you once in the Piggly Wiggly about twenty years ago, and I have never forgotten you. I was with my mom and met you briefly and chatted for a moment or two. You never mentioned God, but His love was flowing out of you in such a way that I have never forgotten that meeting."

She seemed to be taken aback, but she said, "Can I come have lunch with you? I want to spend time with you."

I assured her that we would love to have her join us.

We sat in the church where dinner had been prepared and had a wonderful time just talking and enjoying each other. I found out that her full name is Sarah Love McReynolds (yes, her real middle name is Love), and she had worked for years with my Charlie at Virginia Iron Coal and Coke, a strip-mining company. They were great friends, and he ***loved*** her. I told her that she had to be a part of the reason that Grandad had come to Jesus. I'm so glad that Charlie had someone like her to show him what true Christianity is. People like her are rare, indeed.

As our time together was drawing to an end, I told Sarah that I believed God had arranged that day's events so that she would know how proud He was of her and the way she lived her life. In a very precious and humble way, she said, "I think so, too."

You see, I believe one of the greatest compliments we ever give God is to truly feel secure in His love and to truly believe that He is very proud of us. I often tell a story about my dear daughter, Becca, that illustrates this in the same way that Sarah's story does. When Becca was about two or three years old, I was bathing in the bathroom that is connected to my bedroom. The floor in that bedroom squeaked every time you stepped on a certain part of it. I heard that squeak and said, "Who is that in my room?" And in a very sweet but confident voice, she answered, "It's Becca, the one you love so much!"

I just melted with love for my baby and gratitude that she knew her momma loved her like that. It made me feel that I had done something right as a mother. I think that's how God must feel when he sees that we know we're loved and are confidently walking in that truth.

Sarah and I hugged, and I watched that wonderful servant of God walk away. God had surely given me a special treat on such a sad day. My son, Scott, (he's my comedian) was standing there with me and he said, "After meeting her, I'm thinking, 'Why try'?" She was so full of God's Spirit that just being in her presence made you see what real love should be. We laughed, and I just thought to myself what an awesome and ***sweet*** God we serve.

The Septic Tank Story

Yes, it's called "The Septic Tank Story"—that's not a misprint. In the New Testament, Jesus assures us that "a sparrow doesn't fall to the ground apart from the will of My Father. And even the very hairs on your head are numbered" (Luke 12:6-7), and anyone who knows what kind of hair I have knows that is a miracle in and of itself! If I believed that to be true, then I also had to believe that God knew where my septic tank was buried.

Before my stepdad passed away in 2008, my sister, my mom, and I sat around the kitchen table and discussed Mom's future. At this point, my stepfather had stage four lung cancer and was slipping away from us—both physically and mentally—at an alarming rate. Mom had sought to care for him as best she could, but exhaustion and sleep deprivation were taking their toll. She was very anxious about facing the future alone, so we weighed all our options and decided that if she still felt like she couldn't stay on her own after his passing, then she would sell her house and move in with my family. We would have to build an addition to our house in order for that to happen.

At the time, my sister was in the middle in a Bible study called "The Patriarchs," and her reading for the next day was about Joseph sending for his daddy to come live with him in Egypt during the famine. Joseph was taking care of his father in his old age and wanted him to live in comfort with him. That's exactly what we wanted for our mom. After she had suffered and given so much taking care of her husband, we wanted her older years to be full of comfort and free from worry. We felt like God was confirming our decision by reminding us of the story of Joseph and his father Jacob.

Soon after our discussion around that table, my stepdad passed away. Mom was devastated and didn't feel like she could stay in the house where they shared so many memories. My aunt, a real estate agent, put a for sale sign up in the yard, and the house sold to the first couple that looked at it—a miracle considering how bad the economy was at that time, with the sale of real estate at an all-time low.

The next step was getting an addition built onto our house. I asked a guy at the gym where I worked if he knew a builder, and he gave me the number of a close friend of his. We talked on the phone, and he came over the next day. He was not only a building contractor but also an architect and had excellent ideas about how to create a beautiful and functional space. I wanted her room to be fit for a queen, and he could deliver. He said that he could start the next Tuesday because of a cancellation. Sometimes when God starts to move, all you can do is hold on for the ride. Things were falling into place so quickly that I could hardly keep up.

Some family members talked to Mom and expressed their concern that things might be moving **too** fast. They were suspicious because the contractor had asked for his money up front. God knew I had no idea what I was doing in the construction world, and He and I both knew that I would be easy prey if someone wanted to rip me off. So as I was meeting with God that morning in my quiet time, I asked Him what to do. I was reading in Isaiah 30 at the time, and that morning, verse 21 spoke to me, "Whether you turn to the right or to the left, your ears will hear a voice behind you saying, 'This is the way, walk in it'." I told my Heavenly Father that I needed to hear that voice because I only wanted His will for us and for my mom.

As I opened the gym that morning, one of the ladies who came in had recently had some remodeling done at her house. I knew her to be a very shrewd person who wasn't the easy prey type like me—the perfect person to question about protocol and contractors and such. I described our situation, told her what was in the contract, and asked her if that was apropos. I didn't mention the name of the company being considered—Madex Construction—because it just never came up. She said that everything sounded right, which made me feel a little better.

I went into another room to do my regular morning checklist, making sure that everything was ready for our clients. When I walked out, the lady I'd been speaking with was waiting for me. She told me that her neighbors were having some remodeling done and that they were very happy with the company they'd hired—a company called Madex Construction! There it was—the voice behind me saying, "This is the way, walk in it." As I told her that was the construction company I was considering, one of the other girls said, "Terri's been praying!"

I immediately called Mom and told her, and I also was quick to let my aunt know what was going on. I knew that she loved Mom and was just trying to look out for her, and I didn't want her to worry. To tell you the truth, I really appreciated and completely understood her concern for all of us.

We started construction and almost immediately came up against another roadblock. To get a building permit, I had to know exactly where the septic tank was located. My house had been built nearly twenty years earlier, and like most folks, unless the septic tank backed up, it got very little attention from us. I talked to the person who needed the map showing the location of our septic tank, but although he could suggest someone else I could talk to, he said that he really didn't know what to tell me to guarantee getting my hands on such a map. I called the person he had suggested, leaving a message and then sat down on the couch to talk to God. I told Him that I felt like He had assured me that this was His will and that I knew He could work this impossible situation out for us.

About that time, Rick came home and as we were discussing what we could do, out of the blue he said, "Let's go out and look at it."

I said "Okay," but all the time I was thinking, "*Without x-ray vision, I don't know how this is going to help, but if it will make you feel better, I'll go.*" We walked out into the front yard, and a lady was standing there with a clipboard in her hand. That may sound unusual, but when you're "under construction," you learn that people come and go onto and off of your property a lot. We had gotten so used to it that I just walked up to her and started talking. I told her that we'd found out that in order to get a building permit, we were somehow going to have to come up with a map showing the location of our septic tank. She flipped through the papers on her clipboard and then said, "I have one right here. You can have it."

I was truly flabbergasted, and she could tell. When I told her that she was my "septic tank angel," she replied that she usually didn't have one of those maps with her, but she just "happened" to have ours.

As the old hymn says, "His eye on the sparrow, so I know He watches me . . . ." And I also know that when my God is watching over me, <u>nothing</u> ever just happens.

The Sandwich Story

Jesus says that He won't forget even a cup of cold water given in His Name (Mark 9:41). I am so glad He has included information like that in the Bible because it assures me of His intimacy and care in the details of my ordinary days.

My mom moved in with us after my stepdad passed away in 2008. We had to build an addition onto our home, so we had construction workers at our house almost daily for about six months. One of those workers just tugged at my heartstrings. He was humble and sweet and worked so hard with barely a break for hours on end.

One of those days as I was puttering around the kitchen, I felt like God was prompting me to go and ask that young worker if he would like a drink. The scripture about giving a cup of water to someone in His Name kept running around in my head. As I walked into the room where he was working, I felt like God wanted me to ask him if he'd like a sandwich, too. But I thought to myself, "He's going to think I'm weird, or he's going to think that I think he's too poor to have his own lunch, or that I need to mind my own business, or, or, or . . ." So, instead of paying attention to God's gentle urging, I just smiled and acted normal (I think it's a good thing people can't read minds) and asked if he'd like a drink. He said, "Yes".

I took him the drink, and a few minutes later, he humbly pecked on the door. When I opened it, he said, "Could I have a sandwich, please?"

I felt so bad. Suddenly, I understood why God wanted me to ask him about the sandwich. The Lord knew that he was hungry, and God wanted to preserve his dignity. From that day on, I always fed my construction friend and made sure he had plenty to drink. I call him my "construction friend" because I never found out his name. He didn't speak English very well, and my Spanish was extremely limited, so I just tried to speak the universal language—God's love.

I guess he worked for about a week straight, morning to late evening. I would give him part of our supper, and every time he handed the plate back to me, it looked as if he had washed it because there wasn't a scrap of food left.

On Saturday evenings, we have a family ritual of ordering from a little restaurant called Drums. We love it because they have wonderful, greasy, southern food. My mother-in-law had called in the order on this particular Saturday, and my son Scott and I were headed out the door to pick it up. I suddenly remembered my construction friend and thought to myself that I should have asked before we placed the order if he wanted a sandwich, too. As I was going down my front steps, I said a prayer that God would have them stick an extra sandwich in our bag if He wanted my friend to have one. I didn't even know if he would still be there when we got back.

By the time we picked up the food and got to Memaw's house (she only lives a few houses down from us in the neighborhood), I'm ashamed to admit that in my hungry state, I had forgotten all about my prayer—that is, until Scott pulled out all the sandwiches and passed them around the table. We all had our food, but then Scott pulled out one more sandwich and wanted to know why we had an extra one!

I snapped out of my hungry mode and was suddenly in Holy mode. God didn't forget about His hungry child working at my house. I grabbed that sandwich and felt like the Blues Brothers "on a mission for God." I delivered that BLT "in Jesus' Name." The young man smiled and thanked me (probably thinking I was a little bit nuts).

When his last day at my house came, I knew I hadn't shared the gospel with him, and I couldn't because of the language problem. I didn't know Spanish except for counting to three and didn't think that would help. During my quiet time that morning I asked God to supply me with a Spanish tract, so my friend would know that Jesus was the reason that his strange friend was so nice.

I had a completely full day that particular day but knew that God could deliver a tract if He so chose. I honestly had no idea where I could get one. I had to run to a Christian bookstore that day called Gullions to pick up some books for a friend. People who know me have no trouble believing that I am so forgetful, but I had already forgotten about my "tract prayer"—until I walked by a little display **full** of Spanish tracts. Praise God that He is not limited in any way by forgetfulness. We can pray and go about our business, trusting that He will order our steps during the day and bring across our paths whatever is needed. I asked the owner which one would be good for my friend, and he gave me a whole pack of them and didn't even charge me.

I came home, fed him one last time, and put a tract in the front seat of his truck. I've not seen him again, but since God was obviously after him, I have a feeling I'll see him in heaven. I hope so.

Shelly's Story

Where do I start with Shelly? She is a dear friend and definitely a one-of-a-kind personality. She is confident, honest, beautiful, and she speaks her mind as she follows hard after God.

I met Shelly when a mutual friend of ours brought her to attend a Bible study at my house. She was a little blown away by my honesty, especially my story about writing to the IRS (another story in this book). She sat back and mentally took notes to see if I really believed all the stuff I said. She later confessed to me that she even watched me pray (which, of course, I didn't see at the time, my eyes being shut), because she had no time for insincerity, and she wanted to see if my face told the same story as my words. I guess I passed the test because she came back to Bible study after Bible study.

Over the years, I watched her as she sat in the most comfortable chair in the living room, eagerly hanging onto every word and trying to figure out how to get intimate with the invisible God of the universe. I jokingly told her we would know she had grown spiritually when she didn't arrive early to make sure she got the most comfortable chair. Shelly's not a very emotional person, and the idea that you could have feelings of love for someone you can't see was a concept she found confusing.

Shelly was a potter, and she made some of the most beautiful and unique pieces I had ever seen. In fact, her pottery was in such demand that she had hired two of her good friends to help her keep up.

In 2003, Rick and I were having a really hard time making ends meet, and I started to wonder if I should take a part-time job to help with the bills. As Rick was looking on the internet one Sunday morning for a part-time job to supplement his income, I asked God to show me if He wanted me to get a job. I thought of Shelly and wished that she needed someone, but I knew that she had all the help she needed at the time. So I just left it with God and got ready for church.

When I got to church and walked into the foyer, there was Shelly! She had come to visit our church and wanted to go to Sunday School with me. I was so glad to see her. As we sat down in class, Shelly turned to me and told me that one of her employees had left her suddenly. She was so upset, but I knew that I had just gotten the job I had prayed about only minutes before.

I started asking questions, and Shelly suddenly said, "Do you want to come to work for me?" I told her what I had prayed that morning before coming to church, and she was jubilant—just like I was! She told me that I could work whatever hours that I wanted and that she would accommodate my schedule.

After Sunday School, I went into the sanctuary for worship and sat next to Rick. I told him about my prayer and what had just happened. He said, "Do you want to go to work?"

I said, "I want to be home with the kids, but I would rather go to work than have you work anymore than you do." He had tears running down his sweet face.

The next day, I had to go by the church for something, and on the way home, the pressure of finances, homeschooling, trying to be a wonderful wife, mother, and friend just came crashing down on me. As I sat in the car, I started to cry, telling God that I was overwhelmed. I told Him that I would send my two younger children to Christian Family Academy, a new school that catered to homeschooled kids, ***if*** we could get a scholarship for them. I knew the school had just started, which meant a scholarship would be out of the question, so I dried my tears and decided that I wouldn't whine in the middle of the will of God and that He would give me what I needed.

That night in Bible study, Shelly and I cheerfully shared that I was going to start working for her and how excited we both were. After we finished and everyone had gone home, I got a call from one of my friends who had been there that night. She said, "How are you going to do all of this?"

I said, "I just will."

She then asked, "What about Christian Family Academy?", and I said, "We can't afford it"—to which she replied, "What if you had a scholarship?"

Well, my jaw dropped. I asked her to hold on for a second so I could tuck my daughter quickly in bed—and gather my thoughts—and when I came back to the phone, I told her what I had prayed earlier that day in the car.

God was, indeed, at work. My friend knew of a local charitable organization that focused on doing things for the good of the community, and she said that she knew of nothing better for a community than helping out two parents who were working hard to raise wonderful children and who needed a little assistance.

By the next morning, I had full scholarships for both kids.

I started work at Shelly's, and we talked about God from the time I got there until I would leave. She had so many challenging questions, and she didn't settle for pat answers. We talked a lot about the husband/wife relationship. Shelly had taken my class on Biblical submission to your husband, and while "submissive" was not a word I would have used to describe Shelly, she was convinced that it was the right thing to do.

Shelly desperately wanted to simplify her family's life so she wouldn't have to work so much and could concentrate more on being a wife and mother. I assured her that I believed God wanted the same thing.

At about this same time, she found a house that had been on the market a long time, and the price had dropped dramatically. She told me she thought having that particular house would be the answer for her family. Because the monthly house payment would be lower than the current one, she wouldn't have to work as much. The house had space for her to do her pottery, and it had land for her horses. While it did seem perfect, I told her to pray about it and stay under her husband's authority. God would lead through Richard.

One morning as Shelly was having her quiet time, she asked God if He was ***willing*** to give her this house. She flipped the pages of her Bible over into the New Testament because she thought that she needed to get to know Jesus more, and she saw the heading titled, "The Man with Leprosy." This is what she read: "While Jesus was in one of the towns, a man came along who was covered with leprosy. When he saw Jesus, he fell with his face to the ground and begged Him, 'Lord, If You are **willing**, You can make me clean.' Jesus reached out His hand and touched the man. '**I am willing**,' He said" (Luke 5:12-13a).

Now this particular translation of the Bible prints all the words Jesus spoke in red ink, and when Shelly read those red words, she felt like God was saying them directly to her. When she told me about it, I totally agreed. God speaks to us through His Word. She was so excited and so was I. I love to see women start to discern God's voice for themselves.

I had shared with her that God had given me promises before, and that I would go back and read them again and again as I would sometimes feel insecure or start to doubt. Rereading those promises was reassuring to me.

Later, she told me about sitting in a church service and not getting much out of that particular sermon (I told you she was very honest), so she decided to go back to her promise and read it again. She couldn't remember the exact chapter and verse but she knew it was somewhere in the book of Luke, so she just started searching. As she did so, she came upon another word that she felt God was speaking to her: "Blessed is she who has believed that what the Lord has said to her will be accomplished" (Luke 1:45). When she shared this with me, I could tell God was confirming what He had said. That day, we had revival in that "potter's house" among the clay!

Shelly and Richard put a bid in on the house and much to her horror, two other people also did on the same day. She came into the pottery shop all out of sorts. I told her not to worry because if God had decided to give her that house, it wouldn't matter if Donald Trump put in a bid!

To make a long story short, Shelly, Richard, and their daughter Ashton now live in that house God gave them, and most importantly, Shelly is blessed because "she believed that what the Lord has said to her would be accomplished!"

But there's more: Shelly's new house was located too far away for me to drive there to work every day, and since Shelly would be working fewer hours, she didn't need me as an employee anymore. However, at that same time, financial deliverance came to Rick and me, so I didn't need that job anymore. God's timing is perfect! God had used that job, not for the money, but to show us both that He is trustworthy.

The Ironing Board Story

"Does Job fear God **for nothing**?" is the question that Satan posed to God when God said to him, "Have you considered My servant Job? There is **no one** like him; he is blameless and upright, a man who fears God and shuns evil" (Job 1:8-9a).

You see, Satan has been observing human beings much longer than the best psychologist money can buy. He knows we are all about us, and that it is totally against our nature to serve anyone **for nothing** and that includes God. Even in God's reply we see something very telling: "There is **no one** like him." This is a sad commentary on us humans.

You've read about my "white funeral" (in my story of surrender) that God and I attended years ago. For seven years prior to that funeral, I was "like a wave of the sea, blown and tossed by the wind" (James 1:6). But after that funeral, God started to disciple me. Luke 14:26-27 says:

> "**If** *(*big if*)* anyone comes to Me and does not hate his father and mother, his wife and children, his brothers and sisters—yes, even his own life—he ***cannot*** be My disciple. And anyone who does not carry his cross (go to his own death) and follow Me **cannot** be My disciple" (emphasis mine).

But what I want you to know is that no matter how sincere I was, God couldn't disciple me because I was still in charge. It's an impossibility. When we weigh out total obedience to God against the importance of our family, friends, and most of all ourselves, we will choose self-love or family-love over God every time. We will be like the Pharisees in John 12:42-43:

> "Yet at the same time many even among the leaders believed in Him. But because of the Pharisees *(your mom, dad, children, etc)* they would not confess their faith for fear they would be put out of the synagogue; for they **loved praise** from men **more than** praise from God" (*emphasis mine*).

That ought to run chills up and down all our spines. I see myself there, don't you?

I know you're saying, "I thought this was going to be a cute story about an ironing board." Well, hold on—I'm getting to that.

God uses ordinary things to teach ordinary people, and my ironing board was used to teach me something profound. Jesus said, "He who has an ear, let him hear what the Spirit says . . ." (Rev. 2:7a). This means our ears have to be tuned in by His Spirit to hear what He is trying to teach us through every circumstance. Nothing is haphazard in the life of a saint.

The day I was contemplating writing this story, my daily devotional for October 31st in <u>My Utmost For His Highest</u> was entitled "The trial of Faith" and read as follows:

> *"We have the idea that God rewards us for our faith, it may be so in the initial stages. But we do not earn anything through faith—faith brings us into the right relationship with God and gives Him His opportunity to work. Yet God frequently has to knock the bottom out of your experience as His saint to get you in direct contact with Himself. God wants you to understand that it is a life of faith, not a life of emotional enjoyment of His blessings. The beginning of your life of faith was very narrow and intense, centered around a small amount of experience that had as much emotion as faith in it, and it was full of light and sweetness. Then God withdrew His conscious blessings to teach you to "walk by faith"* (2 Corinthians 5:7). *And you are worth much more to Him now than you were in your days of conscious delight with your thrilling testimony. Faith by its very nature must be tested and tried. And the real trial of faith is not that we find it difficult to trust God, but that God's character must be proven as trustworthy in our own minds. Faith being worked out into reality must experience times of unbroken isolation. Never confuse the trial of faith with the ordinary discipline of life, because*

> *a great deal of what we call the trial of faith is the inevitable result of being alive. Faith, as the Bible teaches it, is faith in God coming against everything that contradicts Him—a faith that says, "I will remain true to God's character whatever He may do." The highest and greatest expression of faith in the whole Bible is—"Though He slay me, yet will I trust Him"* (Job 13:15). (Chambers, 1995)

The words slaying and trusting may sound a little dramatic when I'm telling an ironing board story, but the point of Chambers' devotional is choosing to love and serve God in the absence of His provision or deliverance.

Or when it seems like He's too busy to notice that you're a housewife chasing an ironing board around the kitchen.

The one I had was very old, and one leg was missing the foot part that made it stand up without wobbling, so as I ironed, it kind of swayed and rocked with me. My mother-in-law had given me fifty dollars for my birthday, and I was so excited because I was going to buy a brand-new, state-of-the-art, non-swaying and non-rocking ironing board with my money. Well, I ended up having to use my precious little stash of money to pay a bill or buy groceries, and inside, I felt sad. Life was very difficult for me at this point because no matter how hard I tried, it seemed like we never had enough money for anything beyond the basics. Deep inside each of us, we want to say, "God, I did everything You said! Now pay up and make my life effortless and happy." But God was teaching me how to serve Him **for nothing** except Himself and His **presence**—not His **presents**.

I am so thankful that He didn't pay up in the way I wanted. I would have stayed shallow, prideful, and conceited (which I was and still can be).

As I stood in my kitchen and looked at my gimpy-legged ironing board, I told God that I loved Him and would be happy with that ironing board since He had apparently decided it was what was best for me. I truly meant it and my heart was light and filled with joy because "godliness with contentment is great gain" (1Timothy 6:6). Oh, the joy of letting God map out your life and your days.

Right after my silent conversation with God, the kids and I went for a walk. It was trash pick-up day so everyone had their trash cans at the end of their driveways, and as we walked toward one house, it looked as if the contents of the entire house had been emptied and placed where the trash can should be. As we got closer, I could hardly believe my eyes. There, propped up so that anyone walking by would see it, was an ironing board! A beautiful ironing board! **My** new, beautiful ironing board! God was letting me see the truth of "seek first His kingdom and His righteousness, and all these things will be given to as well" (Matthew 6:33). Can you believe that means an ironing board?

I still use that ironing board and probably will until Jesus takes me home. What a reminder of His provision and love. If He cares about such a simple thing, should I ever worry that He won't take care of everything else that concerns me and all the ones I love?

This story is a little different from my other stories because I'm not actually the writer. It's "Katherine's Story" and she wrote it for me. I was a bit hesitant about asking Katherine if she would mind if I included her story in my book because she is a very quiet and private person. As you read, you will see that I asked Katherine to come to Bible study many years ago, and although aware of the major changes that took place in her life during this time, I didn't know the details until now. Thank you, Katherine, for being vulnerable and honest; it is beautiful . . . .

Katherine's Story

"Therefore, I tell you, her many sins have been forgiven—for she loved much. But he who has been forgiven little loves little." Then Jesus said to her, "Your sins are forgiven."
Luke 7:47-48

"You are evil!" My husband of nearly eleven years directed the cut to me with a snarl as he sat at the kitchen table of our (really **my**) new house. We had been separated for a few months and he had come to pick up our daughter for the weekend.

I did not deign to answer, but merely met his glare with a cold stare that I had perfected to protect myself from verbal attacks. My thoughts; however, ran rampant. "*Who do you think you are?*" I demanded silently. "*How dare you call me names when I am trying to make a life for myself? I have a right to be happy!*" I raged inwardly.

I was used to hiding my emotions, and maintaining self-control. Allowing him to cause me to respond in anger would be a sign of weakness, that I had lost control of the situation. Above all, I must stay in control . . .

The small child peeked around the corner of the back of the house. The woman's face was haggard and tired. Tears rolled down her cheeks as she attempted to silence deep sobs that threatened to overwhelm her. The woman reached down and pulled an item of clothing from the basket and hung it on the line. The child crept forward, wanting to offer comfort, but not knowing how.

One of my most painful childhood memories is of my mother hanging out clothes on the clothesline with tears streaming down her face. My father had verbally abused her to the point where she had broken down. My mother seldom showed her emotions. She was not demonstrative, even to her children, but I knew she felt deeply. Like any good "southern woman," she worked hard to please her man. She spoiled him, probably because she was taught to, but also because he expected it. She worked full time as a teacher, yet she cooked a wholesome meal every night and nurtured five children. After completing her nightly work of household duties, she sat at the dining room table grading papers while my father read a book or went to bed. I never recall my father lifting a hand to assist her in any way with household tasks. Yet my mother never complained about him or the unfairness of a double standard that required that she work full time, but complete all the household chores as well (except what I and my siblings did). As I walked out toward the clothesline, observed her trembling hands and tear stained cheeks, I hated my father for his mistreatment of her. He never, to my knowledge, physically attacked my mother in those days, but his verbal abuse was painful. Both his wife and his children had felt the searing attack of his tongue. If he was in a bad mood, we walked on egg shells and attempted to stay out of his way.

I do not consciously remember making a vow to never let a man treat me that way, but I obviously made that decision. A man, whether he was my husband or not, was not going to treat me as a servant or an inferior. He would respect me, I vowed, or there would be no relationship between us. He would never shout at me or my children.

The girl was a little older, working in the tobacco fields as the hot summer sun beat down. She struggled to manage the hoe, much too big for her small hands, as she attempted to chop weeds from around the young tobacco plants. She kept a wary eye on her father as he plowed nearby. Unexpectedly he stopped the tractor and came storming over to her. Jerking the hoe from her trembling hands he shouted, "Can't you do any better? You are going to kill the plants! This is how you are supposed to do it!" He demonstrated (for the first time) the correct way to achieve the task. "Do you think you can do it right?" he shouted as he thrust the hoe back in her hands and stomped off. Lowering her head to shield her tears from his view, the girl resumed her chore.

★ ★ ★

My husband and I married in 1988 after a four year courtship. We both had failed at marriage previously and were apprehensive about the union. However, we believed that we loved each other, that we knew how to compromise, that labor within a marriage should be distributed fairly, and that we were mature enough to make our marriage succeed. It was only a short time before major problems began. The things which had most attracted us to each other served to create the wedges that drove us apart.

I had greatly admired my husband's creativity and willingness to help others. He is a hard worker and talented in numerous ways. Having retired from the textile industry before I knew him, he spent his time in a variety of jobs, construction, remodeling, repair work, and farming. We seemed to have the same dreams for the future.

My husband admired my independence, my organizational skills, my drive to do my best at tasks, and my ability to view situations objectively. Suddenly, marriage seemed to change our mutual admiration society. It appeared to me that my husband only used his creativity, hard work ethic, and building talents to help ***other*** people. He never seemed to have the time or inclination to do the tasks that I viewed as important for our family. I resented how active he was in our church because that work took him away from what I viewed as his family obligations. The dreams that we had for the future remained just that, dreams; his promises never became the reality, just empty conversation. His income was limited and went to pay for his own personal needs; he was not able to contribute to any of the household or family expenses. I was angry that I worked full time and paid all the household bills, yet he did little (from my point of view) in regard to household chores.

Likewise, my organizational skills irritated him because I tried to organize ***him***! My ambition led me to further my education and to seek teaching jobs at the college level. I became more involved in my career and less attentive to my husband and family. My ability to treat situations objectively led me to emotionally distance myself from a marriage that I viewed as constraining and financially burdensome. Our marriage, fragile from the onset, now seemed doomed to failure.

Following completion of a PhD, I was offered a college teaching job 125 miles from home. My husband was reluctantly supportive, only because he knew my determination to take the job. I believe he thought that I would have ended our marriage immediately if he opposed me. He, at least, viewed his marriage vows with strong commitment, while I seemed ready to abandon my pledge to him. Within a year, I had purchased a house and moved my children to new schools in a different county. We went "home" every week-end to visit our husband/father at our "other" house.

Very quickly after I had taken the job I met a man with whom I developed a close friendship. He seemed to be everything my husband was not. He enjoyed going places, he took me out to eat, he loved to travel and he treated me with kindness at all times. Thankfully I was never physically unfaithful to my husband. I was not sexually intimate with my man-friend. However, I was emotionally unfaithful to my marriage vows and my relationship with my husband continued to deteriorate.

The little girl was now a middle aged woman. It was 1998 and she was at her father's hospital beside. He was dying after a series of strokes and a long period of declining health. She stared at him in silence, having purposely come to visit him in private. "Daddy, I do not know why you were so angry all the time, why you treated us all so badly. I want to forgive you. I want you to find some happiness. I pray you will find peace with God. I love you."

Those words were very hard for me to say. I wanted them to be true even as I realized that they were not. I did not want him to die without me saying the words. However, I continued to carry the legacy of his anger. His long illness had been an unpleasant time, requiring that all his children (as well as their spouses) assist in caring for him. He became physically abusive until his strength ebbed entirely. The stress upon my mother and our entire family was tremendous. My father's death was in the middle of the downward spiral of my marriage.

⋆ ⋆ ⋆

"The Spirit of the Lord is on me, because he has anointed me to preach good news to the poor. He has sent me to proclaim freedom for the prisoners and recovery of sight for the blind, to release the oppressed, to proclaim the year of the Lord's favor."

Isaiah 61:1-2a; Luke 4:18-19

The Lord is faithful, even when we are not. Somehow, even though I was most undeserving, he reached down to me, although perhaps not in the way I would have chosen. My marriage was ending and I thought God was guiding me to a permanent relationship with my man-friend. We were both lonely and seeking a relationship. However, God had other plans for me. He was guiding me toward what was to become the hardest trial of my life.

In January of 1999, I took off my wedding ring and announced to my husband that I was leaving him. On the week-ends that I went "home" I stayed with my mother to avoid being with my husband. Other times, he would come and pick up our daughter, thus occurred many angry conversations such as the one in which he labeled me "evil."

Suddenly my life crashed around me. My man-friend rejected me with the statement, "I want no part of breaking up a marriage!" (I wondered what he thought he had been doing previously.) I was shattered—my marriage was destroyed and my hopes for the future dissipated completely. I sunk into depression. During my lowest point, I collapsed across my bed and cried out to the Lord. "God, what have I done?" I realized that Satan's temptations had brought me down and I was totally in the wrong in regard to what had occurred in my marriage. I had tried to rationalize my sin based on my own selfish desires. I begged God's forgiveness and pleaded for his guidance.

That same week, as I was working in my yard (I loved my yard, it was my therapy), a neighbor whom I did not know approached. She lived directly across the street and we had waved at each other, but had not become acquainted. After an exchange of greetings, she invited me to a Bible study that she was to begin shortly. Opening my mouth to decline, I heard a voice inside my head say, "**You need to do this**." When my response emerged, it was an affirmative. A smile lit her face and she promised further details as she departed. As I watched her leave, I wondered if I had done the right thing. I am a shy and reserved person, and knew I would not feel comfortable in a group of strangers. However, I felt God was answering my plea for guidance and had sent my neighbor as his messenger. Her name was Terri.

★ ★ ★

The Bible study was "Me Obey Him!" After the first session I went back across the street to my house and cried out to the Lord, "My Lord, what are you doing to me?" There could have been no greater shock to me than learning of the expectation that I was to submit to my husband. The Lord could not have chosen a more reluctant participant than I to teach his lesson. After reading the first chapter of our study book I was ready to flush it down the toilet, tear out each page and burn it individually, or stuff it into a bottle and toss it into the ocean for some other victim to discover. I could hear God chuckling—obviously He has a sense of humor!

But, I persevered, I studied the Bible, I prayed and those loving women prayed with me and for me. God wrapped his loving arms around me and said, **"I will be with you."** He sent his angel of mercy, Terri, to help me through the rocky time and a group of "angel helpers" to support my baby steps toward freedom. At last I was able to see my husband as the partner God had chosen for me. I recognized the gift that God had given me when he saved our marriage. For the first time in our marriage, we were able to move toward a partnership, rather than an ongoing struggle for control. I put my wedding ring back on (my husband had never removed his).

After completing "Me Obey Him," I joined another Bible study with Terri. This one was "Breaking Free" with Beth Moore. During this study, I was finally able to begin to let go of the bondage that had entrapped me since childhood. For the first time, I was able to recognize that I was choosing to be enslaved by my terrible memories of my father's dominance. By giving the burden to my Lord and Savior, Jesus Christ, I was finally released from oppression and able to live in freedom.

The reader should not believe that my father was always a terrible person. I had some good memories, but the problem was that the bad ones entrapped me and held me in bondage. My father was enslaved by his own demons. Having lived through the Great Depression and served in World War II, he had expected a better life when he returned from war and settled on a farm in rural North Carolina. However, a disagreement with his family and a few hard, lean years of harvest seemed to shatter his dreams. He may have always been a hard and angry man who took out his frustrations on his family, but I want to believe that he cherished my mother and loved his children, but was never able to express it. I hope he has found peace.

★ ★ ★

It is now 2010. Certainly our marriage has not been without bumps, but my husband and I are traveling the road together, as partners, as two joined. I love him, respect him, and honor him (not sure I have the obey part yet!) Praise God for his mercy! My Lord has forgiven me much and I love much.

★ ★ ★

Epilogue

During Katherine's walk of faith, she began to write a Christian novel, *Sheltered by an Angel's Wings*. Although a work of fiction, the story was strongly impacted by Katherine's journey of faith on a hard and rocky road. You may learn more about *Sheltered by and Angel's Wings* at www.katherinepasour.net or on Facebook at shelteredbyanangel'swings.

Kenny's Story

Although this is called "Kenny's Story", it's really a story of God's mercy. I never got to know Kenny very well and decided not to ask his friends and family lots of questions about him because I don't think it's important. This situation is a wonderful example of the lyrics from the song "Mercy Came Running" (Phillips, Craig and Dean, 1998). My favorite line is, "When I could not reach mercy, mercy came running to me."

Kenny found out in 2010 that he didn't have long to live because he had a liver disease. Years of drug and alcohol abuse had caught up with him and wreaked havoc on his body. He was only 55. My friend, Vickie Vaughan, is a close friend of Kenny's mother, Nadine. Nadine was beside herself with worry and fear for Kenny's physical life, but she was terrified because of his spiritual life. She knew he was not saved and she was desperate for someone to share with him how to become a child of God before it was too late. Vickie asked me if I would go with her to talk to him, and, of course, I said I would. I'm not used to talking to people that I don't know at all about Jesus, but I was willing. My pastor always says that courage is not the absence of fear, but saying "no" to your fear and "yes" to God. I've learned that as God's child, I just need to go ahead and say "yes" and trust that He has paved the way.

On the day Vickie and I were supposed to visit Kenny, Vickie called to let me know that Kenny's wife had a relative who was a preacher, and that this preacher was going to talk to Kenny. I have to admit, I was relieved.

With that out of the way, I was looking forward to Wednesday, when I would be getting together with a writers' club I had joined. We met once a week to share our writings, give each other tips, and critique one another's work. But about lunchtime on Wednesday, I got a phone call from Vickie, telling me Kenny hadn't responded to the visit from the preacher. The minister had brought someone else with him, and Kenny had been kind, but just didn't seem to "get it" as they shared. I'm sure they were part of God's plan, but I've found through the years that what Paul said in Corinthians 3:6 is so true, "I planted the seed, Apollos watered, but God made it grow." He lets many of us do the work, but when someone is born again, it's obviously a miracle from God. No human can open the eyes of another human to the spiritual world; that's a business only God is in. We can share the good news, but that's all: only God can save a soul.

When Vickie asked me if I could meet her to go to Kenny's house, I quickly changed my plans and told her I would. I asked her if he knew we were coming and she said that he didn't. Vickie and I met, got in the car, and headed to his house. We knocked on the door and his wife let us in. I went into the living room, and precious Kenny was lying on his couch, covered with a small blanket, looking very weak and tired. Vickie introduced us and I jokingly said, "Are you feeling bombarded?" I then continued by saying, "I'm here to talk to you about God." I've come to the place in my life of trying to be up front with people because I prefer that myself. I trust someone more if they just tell me the truth. I told Kenny I would only share if he wanted me to, and Vickie said the same. He told me he wanted to hear what I had to say.

I started to share my testimony with him. I told him what a liar, cheat and rebel I had been. I told him that my own choices had cost me so much and I had no one to blame but myself. I told him about leaving Rick, being involved with someone else, exactly what I called myself when I told God that I was desperate for Him to let me find Him. When I got honest with God on that level, He had come to my rescue. When I could not reach mercy, mercy came running to me, and I wanted to make sure I made it clear to Kenny that Mercy would come running to him, too. Vickie could tell that Kenny was "getting it" as I talked.

I began by telling Kenny that in order to go to heaven, you have to be as good as God. There is nothing that equals God except God. We are all sinners, and only one Person had ever lived a perfect life and that was Jesus. Extending both hands to represent a scale, I told Kenny to imagine God on one side of that scale. On the other side of the scale, there was me, a sinner who was lost with no hope, and because of that, the two sides could never balance. No matter how hard I tried, on my own I could never be righteous like God. But since Jesus had lived that perfect life and then died and rose again, ***He*** could come and live in me **if** I would admit what a sinner I was and ask Him to come and save me. My only hope was that the Holy Spirit would come live in my body, which the Bible actually calls a 'temple!' With my Lord and Savior, in the person of the Holy Spirit, living within me, now the two sides of the scale could balance. God Himself would be in me. Wow! What a Savior! I told Kenny that the Bible calls this being "born again." I get to become a new person. Jesus hung on a cross and became sin so that I could become the righteousness of God.

I looked at Kenny and said, "Does that make sense?"

He said, "It makes perfect sense."

I said, "Do you want to be born again?"

He said, "Yes."

I looked at his wife who had sat there silently as we talked and asked her if she had been born again. Tears were streaming down her sweet face, and she shook her head and quietly said, "No."

I said, "Do you want to be?"

She nodded that she did.

I led them both in a simple prayer and they prayed with childlike faith.

After we prayed, Kenny just let out a huge sigh as if the world had been lifted from his shoulders. He hadn't said much at all since we had been there. Now the words came. He said that he couldn't sleep at all the night before and had told his wife that he needed to get his soul right. He then told me that he had asked God to send someone to him to help him understand how to come to God. Whew! "When I could not reach mercy, mercy came running to me." At times like that, I'm so glad I was so rotten because other people who have done horrible things know that they are not too far gone for the grace of God. That's probably why Kenny didn't relate to the preacher. He needed a bigger sinner and that was me. Oh, how I praise God for the freedom to tell the truth about myself and that God promises to use all of it for my good and His glory. I still don't understand how He does it but will just revel in the fact that He does.

We all had a glorious time, and I told Kenny that it was now safe to die. He didn't have to be afraid anymore. We all hugged and cried, and Vickie and I left. I got to see Kenny one more time right around Christmas. He was so sweet, and it was a joy to visit. Before we left, Vickie, Kenny's brother, Kenny, and I stood and held hands and I prayed. It was a precious time and the last time I was to see him. He went home to be with his Lord just a few weeks later.

As I was thinking of Kenny the morning of his funeral and how he truly got into heaven at the eleventh hour, I opened my Bible, as I do every morning and started reading where I had left off the day before. My daily reading was from the book of Matthew 20:1-16, and I read:

> *"For the kingdom of heaven is like the landowner who went out early in the morning to hire men to work in his vineyard. He agreed to pay them a denarius for the day and sent them into his vineyard. About the third hour he went out and saw others standing in the marketplace doing nothing. He told them, 'You also go and work in my vineyard, and I will pay you whatever is right'." So they went.*
>
> *"He went out again about the sixth hour and ninth hour and did the same thing. About the eleventh hour he went out and found still others standing around. He asked them, 'Why have you been standing here all day doing nothing?'*
>
> *"'Because no one has hired us,' they answered.*
>
> *"He said to them, 'You also go and work in my vineyard.'*
>
> *"When evening came, the owner of the vineyard said to his foreman, 'Call the workers and pay them their wages, beginning with the last ones hired and going on to the first.'*
>
> *"The workers who were hired about the eleventh hour came and each received a denarius. So when those came who were hired first, they expected to receive more. But each one of them also received a denarius. When they received it, they began to grumble against the landowner. 'These men who were hired last worked only one hour,' they said, 'and you have made them equal to us who have borne the burden of the work and the heat of the day.'*
>
> *"But he answered one of them, 'Friend, I am not being unfair to you. Didn't you agree to work for a denarius? Take your pay and go.*

> *I want to give the man who was hired last the same as I gave you. Don't I have the right to do what I want with my own money? Or are you envious became I am generous?'*
>
> *"So the last will be first, and the first will be last."*

When I get to heaven, I won't be upset at all that Kenny got the same amount of grace as me. The price Jesus paid for any of us to be saved is His own life and His precious blood. I don't think any of us will be upset about "fairness" when we get to heaven. We'll just be glad to be there. I have gotten to work much longer for God on this earth than Kenny, but that doesn't change the fact that I was just a hungry beggar that told another beggar where to find bread . . . the Bread of Life.

THE "SCREW YOU, DUDE" STORY

I tried to think of a better title for this story, but it is what it is. I talked to God about this as you will see, so I figured if I wrote those words in my prayer journal to The One Who Sits on The Throne in heaven, then my readers could handle it. You see, I talk to God about everything. He sees all and knows all, so I don't have to pretty things up to bring them to Him all day every day and invite Him into every single situation, no matter how ugly or distressing. He knew every word that would ever come out of my mouth, every act of love and obedience, and every sin I would ever commit before I was ever born, and yet He chose me and loves me. What a relief to know that neither I nor my kids disappoint Him or shock Him! He knows it all and always has a plan in place if I will keep my face turned toward Him. What a relief to also know my heart and my home are open and laid bare to Him and He longs to wow me and thrill me with who He is at every turn. As Oswald Chambers says, He intends for life to become one great romance—a glorious opportunity of seeing wonderful things all the time.

Before I started teaching my own Sunday school class, I would do a ten minute devotional in my former class. I would always share things that God was teaching me each week on my own journey. I figured we are all basically the same, and that whatever internal and external things I was dealing with, to some extent, everyone else was also.

Hence, "The Screw You, Dude Story" was born. In 2009, as my family was glued to the television each Tuesday night watching "American Idol," something slightly traumatic happened at the Broome house. The final two contestants were chosen as the finale drew close and my Becca was happy because it was her two favorites, Adam Lambert and Chris Allen. Well, she went straight to Facebook and posted how happy she was. Immediately, one of her friends commented on her post saying, "You like gay people, you're weird!"

We have more than one computer in the house, so my son Andrew was on another computer and typed immediately, "Screw you, dude!"

Becca went through the hall high fiving him or something like that because she was happy her big brother had taken up for her and said something she had thought but never would have typed. Andrew was in college by this time, so he had obviously become accustomed to letting stuff like that fly. I'm not proud; I'm just telling it like it happened.

When Andrew returned to his computer, he discovered that a person from our church had responded to his Facebook posting, chastising him for typing, "Screw you dude." He walked into the living room and said, "Mom, I know I shouldn't have said that, it was wrong, but that is exactly what I can't stand about church people. That lady is mad because I said what I did, but she could care less that someone just threw away a whole group of people." He meant gay people, of course. He proceeded to tell me that it wasn't a Christian contest, it was a talent contest and that Adam Lambert (the gay one) was the better talent.

The Bible plainly condemns homosexuality, but listen to the entire passage of scripture where that is contained. "Do you not know that the wicked will not inherit the kingdom of God? Do not be deceived: Neither the sexually immoral nor idolaters nor adulterers nor male prostitutes nor homosexual offenders nor thieves nor the greedy nor drunkards nor slanderers nor swindlers will inherit the kingdom of God" (1 Corinthians 6:9-10).

I have homosexual friends, and they are truly some of the kindest people I know, and I love them dearly. They are not professing Christians but are nicer than many professing Christians. That has put me in a quandary at times because I just hate to know that they are not going to heaven. I felt like God taught me something about this and I will try to explain. As with all my other revelations about things, check them out with the Word because I am just human, and the only book that is one hundred percent truth is the Bible.

I'm very simple in the way I study the Bible and I'm no theologian, but I'm not intimidated by that because I have The Holy Spirit in me and I can read the book that He wrote—the Bible. He is able to teach me the true meaning of scripture as I'm able to comprehend it as long as I get rid of my preconceived, know-it-all tendencies (that we all have).

There are two groups of people in this world, and every reader is in one of these camps; one is 'wicked' and the other is 'righteous'. These labels don't represent so much what you **do** as who you **are**. In Romans 3:10, the Bible plainly states that "There is no one righteous, not even one . . . ." We are all born with a terrible problem; we are sinners. Sinful blood flows through our veins, and sinful thoughts run through our minds. If you doubt what I'm saying, I will pose a question to you that I posed to my Sunday school class. "What if every thought you had on a Sunday morning was put on the big screen for just a ten minute period? How many of you would show up?" Not one single hand was lifted. That's exactly what God sees 24/7. Is anyone feeling righteous now?

Righteousness equals God—period. He is, and we are not. The only righteousness we have any hope of attaining is His righteousness. The great news of the gospel is that God will come and live in a sinner who repents and asks Him to move in. His Spirit will make His home inside of your spirit, and that is how you become righteous—God in you. Of course, you can't fool God, so unless true repentance is there, you don't trick God into coming inside of you. He is the only One that you will never ever manipulate. If He truly comes into your spirit, then the Bible calls that being born again. You are now born again and you are a saint instead of a sinner. It's so simple and yet so profound. If God's Spirit moves into you, there will be evidence of that happening. It may be a slow process, but you will start to partake of the Divine Nature. Your sinful nature will start to be replaced by the Divine Nature. You can actually live by the power of God's Spirit instead of following your sin nature. Oh, the gift that God offers us is unthinkable! I'm not making this up. Listen to what 2 Peter 1:4 says, "Through these He has given us His very great and precious promises, so that through them you may ***participate*** in the Divine Nature and escape the corruption caused by evil desires."

So to put the question of homosexuality in its simplest terms: God is not homosexual, so if He lives in you, you won't keep practicing homosexuality. God in you will rebel against all sin, especially sexual sin. Corinthians 5 says that all other sins are committed outside the body, but sexual sin involves the physical act of putting something that doesn't belong inside the temple where God dwells. That's frightening. No matter how acceptable the rest of the world may find any sexual act outside of marriage, if you are a believer, think about what you are doing each time you engage in sex with your body. It's so serious that I don't think I can put it on paper accurately.

However, temptation is not sin. So if you are a homosexual and tempted to engage in a homosexual relationship, then that is no different than a man or woman who is tempted to sleep with someone of the opposite sex outside of marriage. Sin is sin. God has a standard that no one can keep. That's why He puts Himself in us and then tells us how to behave. He is speaking to the Life in us, not to what we are humanly capable of.

Until you are surrendered to God and filled with His Spirit, you are not living. Your need for intimacy is still there, and sexual oneness is the closest thing to the emotional fulfillment of oneness with God that human beings can achieve. That's why people are obsessed with sex. It is everywhere. Since we don't want to be filled with the Spirit but we still have an obsessive longing for oneness with someone, we chase a poor substitute. Sex is meant to fulfill us and give us pleasure, God's way, in the covenant of marriage. But if you are married and not filled with God's Spirit, sex won't even be as fulfilling as it was meant to be. God meant for us to love each other from the abundance of His love flowing through us.

Christians like to get upset about homosexuality, but you rarely hear them get that upset about the other sins listed in that verse. Is it possible that they might hit too close to home? Some of the other sins listed in that same passage are adultery (need we look any further than the pulpit for this one in far too many cases?), thieves (tax evader comes to mind), greedy ("never touch ***my*** money"), drunkards, slanderers (oh my, what if we listened to phone conversations of others during the week?), and swindlers (people just trying to use you for some reason). All of us deal with most of these things to one degree or another, but a true Christian will go to God and wrestle through prayer for deliverance from our own wretchedness. All of us will slip and fall at times, but that should produce humility so we won't depend on ourselves to any degree, depending instead on God's Spirit for deliverance. As long as we are in these bodies, we will be tempted. It's very humbling to confess that to people because we are so proud and like to think we are above certain things. Here's a newsflash for all of us: we're not.

If any of these sins are things we just embrace and live in without conscience about it, then we need to have a Holy Spirit check. If He is in you, He hates sin—all sin. You will even start to hate the sins that no one but you and God know about that are only in your heart and mind. You start to hunger and thirst for righteousness. As a human made in God's image, you will never feel at home in your own body until it is coursing with the life of God, full and robust. All other pleasures pale completely in comparison. The sad part is that you won't know this unless you give your entire self to Him without reservation. For the homosexual, the great fear is that God won't be enough, and every hope of intimacy is gone if they give up their lifestyle for the unknown. I feel very sorry for them and I'm glad I didn't have to choose. I may not have had the courage either. As a heterosexual, you can have Christ and a sexual, intimate relationship through marriage. We shouldn't be so quick to throw stones. We should minister with tenderness and love. The cost is great for them.

As our American Idol drama continued to unfold, Becca went to bed in tears saying that if we don't tell homosexuals about God's love, who will? We talked and hugged (she cries easily when tired). After a good night's sleep, both kids kind of put the whole episode out of their mind. I eagerly went to God the next morning to discuss the whole matter. I sat on the front porch and started writing in my prayer journal. I laid the whole thing out to God and simply asked Him what He thought about what Andrew did. I said that I knew the "screw you dude" part was wrong (yes, I actually wrote that down), but I said,

"What about Andrew's heart and his anger about throwing away gay people as if they don't matter?"

I finished my Bible reading that day and picked up a book by Catherine Marshall called Beyond Ourselves. The following is what I read that morning. It begins with a group of ministers that were gathered for a retreat.

> *They had gathered for a two-day retreat at a church in New Jersey to discuss mutual problems and to pray about them. As so often happens, the discussion part predominated. It was late afternoon of the final day when a startling event occurred.*
>
> *Suddenly the door of their meeting-room opened and a stranger walked in. The minister of the host church knew him, had seen him often around the neighborhood. Self-consciously the man seated himself at the fringe of the circle. Though there was no more than a momentary pause in the discussion, the experienced eyes of the other clergymen present took in the situation—the watery eyes, the sagging shoulders, the seedy clothing. Obviously the man was an alcoholic.*
>
> *The discussion continued, while the stranger listened. "It seems to me," a crisp voice said, "that all we have been talking about these two days can be summed up in our need for God's power—the kind of power that changes lives, heals, restores, that . . . ."*
>
> *"That's it! That's what I need. I could use some of that."*
>
> *There was sudden silence. While everyone watched, his bleary eyes filled a bit more and the quavering voice continued.*
>
> *"My name is Ernie. I drink too much. People have tried to help me . . . doctors, hospital, clinics, missions, and all that. But I . . . I can't seem to stop. How do I get this power you're talking about?"*
>
> *The question hung, quivering in the silence. Despite the fact that these men were experienced in dealing with people in need, the intrusion was embarrassing. There was a time schedule for the meeting, trains and planes to be caught, families to get back to, next Sunday's sermons to think about. Closing time was at hand.*
>
> *Finally, a white-haired man spoke up. "Ernie, all of us have problems too. It's a problem-filled world . . ." The voice of the elderly minister was gentle, suave, as he sought to identify with the stranger. All of the men knew that the pastor who was speaking had had professional training in counseling.*

> *"As to how we can get God's help. Well, that isn't always too easy. It takes patience, time. There are many roads to God, many avenues by which . . ."*
>
> *"Damn!" The interruption was explosive, passionate.*
>
> *"Damn . . . Damn . . . Damn . . . Damn!"*
>
> *The quiet of the room was suddenly being blasted by Ted, a young minister and a former businessman, anger and impatience written clearly on his face. Again and again he beat his fist down on the seat of the empty chair beside him.*
>
> *"This man doesn't want to hear about our problems," Ted said vehemently. "He's asked us a question—how can he get God's help to stop drinking? We haven't answered him. If we don't know the answer, then let's adjourn this meeting, stop our endless talking, go home and tell our people that the church hasn't any answers for today. In that case, we'd better stop being hypocrites and shut the church doors for good."*
>
> (Marshall 1961, p. 49-51)

The story goes on to tell of Ernie's salvation and the thawing out of the ministers' hearts as they watched God's power change a person. They had spoken of power, now they witnessed it.

Reading that little story showed me that God did honor Andrew's heart of anger toward the accepted hatred and belittling of gay people as unimportant and unloved by God. It was awe-inspiring to see God answer so quickly, and I couldn't wait to tell the kids. I love it when God gives us all glimpses into His heart and mind. You cannot put God in a box. He wants us to know Him intimately and not just listen to everyone's idea of what He is like based on their own biases and hatred of people and things.

My kids don't have quite the overly-excitable personality that I do, but I can tell that they take to heart what I tell them when I feel as if I've heard from God. Watching God answer me and work in our lives as a family has given all my precious children a hunger and thirst for God. Children don't have the baggage of grown-ups, and they recognize their Creator in us if we will unleash Him in our lives and homes. They also spot hypocrisy a mile away, and we parents can, and often will, ruin our children's spiritual lives 'in Jesus' Name'. What a tragedy.

I started to feel like God may want me to share my 'screw you dude' experience with my Sunday school class, so I went to praying about it. To share two ugly words with a Baptist crowd might get me somewhere close to stoning. I wasn't out to offend anyone, so I asked God to show me if He really wanted me to share this whole thing in my little ten-minute time period. I sent up a prayer saying something like, "If you want me to share this, let something come into my life today that addresses homosexuality." I knew that would be somewhat of a miracle since it was a Saturday and all I had planned to do all day was clean the house and not go out the front door except to maybe shake a rug. After my prayer, my mom walked out of her bedroom and asked me to take a look at something in a book she was reading. It was a book by Sheila Walsh called, Honestly. Sheila Walsh, from the "700 Club", had gone into the hospital and was in the psych ward because she had had something akin to a nervous breakdown. Let me share the portion she asked me to read.

SOWING AND REAPING

> *When we find flaws, we find it hard to walk with one another for the duration of the journey. Too often we leave a trail of bodies behind us. I think of situations when friends of mine were in trouble and I believed it was my duty to them and to the Lord to help pull them up by their bootstraps. Based on what appeared to be happening on the outside, I made some quick judgment calls.*
>
> *If someone lets us down, we walk away. This happened to me. What was most painful was that I knew I had done the very same thing to a friend when she needed me. She was one of my few good friends. We went on trips together, sat for hours talking over endless cups of coffee. We laughed and cried as we shared our hopes and dreams for the future. Then one day she sat me down and told me that she thought she was gay. My first question was, "Does your husband know?"*
>
> *Yes, he did. I was absolutely stunned. I had naively assumed that this issue never reared its head among Christians. My friend was taking a risk telling me, reaching out to me for some kind of support—not endorsement, but a sign that I was still her friend.*

And when she needed me most, I was not there. All I could think of was she must be telling me because she is interested in pursuing that kind of relationship with me. I ran for miles. She was a friend in trouble, and I abandoned her.

Now, years later, I sat in the doctor's office in the hospital with tears rolling down my cheeks. I felt crushed and thrown away.

"What is on your mind, Sheila?" he asked.

"I thought these people were my friends," I said. The people I was speaking of were those who had just walked away from me when my life had started to unravel. They were the people who had put an unsympathetic twist on my "breakdown." Was Satan really using me to attack CBN? Was "heaven" really "not pleased with me"?

Once I entered the hospital, more rumors had begun flying. The evangelical world is a fairly small place, and news, especially bad news, travels fast. Bits and pieces of these rumors had been getting back to me, and I was stunned by them. All of them were untrue: from "she's had an affair" to "she's been hallucinating and seeing flying things." And some people—friends—were believing these stories without even talking to me.

"I can't believe some of the things that are being said about me. It makes me wonder if we were ever friends at all."

I was angry and I was hurt, but I did not know what to do. I knew that God had brought me to the hospital to give me an opportunity to look at my life and make some changes. It was hard enough dealing with what was true without trying to extinguish false fires.

The doctor said, "Why don't you go back to your room and talk to the Lord about this. Write out how you feel."

I sat down at my desk very angry. I wrote down the names of the people who had most hurt me. As I sat there, another name came to mind: the friend I had walked away from. I tried to push that thought away; that was not the point of today's exercise, or so I thought. But it became very clear to me that my reaction to her was exactly the point. I tried to reason it away—our circumstances were so different—but the Holy Spirit would have none of that. The fact remained that I was now reaping in my own life what I had sown in another's life. Perhaps if I had been more gracious in the past when

> *my friend had needed me, then I would be experiencing more grace in my own life when I needed it so badly.*
>
> *My friend needed to know, as she struggled with the sin and pain in her own life, that she had a companion in the journey. But I had refused to be there for her. As I allowed this realization to flood over me, I was horrified by what I had done. I wrote her a letter that day, telling her that I understood now what I had done to her. I asked for her forgiveness. I knew that she might not even acknowledge my letter, but I also knew that I had to do whatever it took to confess that I seriously wronged her.*
>
> *Within a few days, she wrote back to me, forgiving me for what I had done. Her letter was gracious and magnanimous. She truly forgave me. It was my first lesson in forgiveness* (Walsh, 1996, p.126-129).

Wow! What a confirmation that I was to share.

I told the kids this story also. Scott said, "For the first time, I'd like to go to Sunday school with Mom!"

Sunday morning came and off I went. I got up and shared that I was going to speak about a group of people that church people think it's ok to malign . . . the homosexual. I shared in detail, spelling the ugly words so as not to offend any further than necessary. I didn't get very much feedback (maybe due to shock, since this was obviously not your ordinary Sunday School lesson), but I didn't get thrown out either, and hopefully some hearts were surprised and opened to the love of God.

As I was finishing writing this story, I couldn't think of a clever way to end it, so I stopped and said a prayer that God would help me end it in a good way. I didn't get anything great so I just ended it with that last period in the previous paragraph. I pushed 'save' on the computer and thought I was done. I didn't realize that God had me pray that prayer because He wanted to put the final period on this story.

Scott walked up to me, not having any idea what I had just finished writing, and said, "I want to show you a cool video." I thought it was going to be a music video, but as this precious young man (in the video) started to talk, I sat mesmerized and stunned as I watched God put His seal of approval on what I had just written and throw down His mighty

"Amen". When God finishes a story, it will leave you breathless. I hope all of you will take the time to watch it.

Simply go to Youtube and type in the name of the video below:

P4CM Presents I Promised I Wouldn't Tell! by Featured RHETORIC Poet J "O" Speaks

The Hat Story

My father-in-law, Jim Broome ("Tataw" to the family), was one of the most moral men I have ever known. He paid his bills on time, took care of his family, defended his family, and always tried to do the right thing. I admired and loved him so very much.

When I re-married Rick, my husband and Tataw's son, I think Tataw was a little suspicious and wary of the huge change in my life. Someone once said, "A new Christian ought to be locked up for the first year," and maybe that wouldn't have been such a bad idea for me. Tataw didn't understand my newfound "overnight religion," but he was always respectful and kind. He got to watch me try so hard to get my wobbly Christian feet under me and learn to walk with Christ. It wasn't pretty or always smooth, but I was trying. Sitting with the family at the supper table one night, Tataw said, "I just don't believe in overnight religion." I felt he was trying to tell me that I was probably deceived and would get over what I had experienced. Well, thank goodness I didn't "get over" it, which meant that Tataw got to see overnight religion for fifteen years.

Those years were wonderful as I watched Memaw (Jim's wife and my mother-in-law) and Tataw and learned about being a family. The respect and love they had for their family and each other quietly discipled me and helped me to love my husband and children more deeply. An added bonus was having lots of laughs and hours of fun because Memaw and Tataw were very funny people!

But during those years, I always prayed for Tataw because although he was a wonderful person, I didn't know if he knew Christ. Who could witness to him? He was a much better person than I, a much better person than most people I knew for that matter. How could I convince him that he was a sinner who needed a Savior? To put it bluntly, I was afraid of his rejection if I broached the subject. Thank God, He still works in the middle of my insecurity and cowardice.

Then in 1998, the news came that Tataw had cancer. In addition to sadness, I felt so panicked! How could I live if this man, who had truly been a father to me, died without Christ! His own righteousness was better than many others, but it wouldn't get him into heaven. I was praying in earnest now. Tataw wasn't a large man physically, but he was a large man inside with a powerful presence. We all felt a certain awe in his presence. It was devastating to watch him struggle with the illness, the fear, and the loss of his masculinity. Who was "man" enough to visit this man and tell him of Christ?

He had many victories and defeats as he fought with all of his heart against that insidious disease, but after about four years, it was obvious that the cancer was going to win . . . physically anyway. It may consume our bodies, but it can't touch the only part of us that will matter in the end: our souls. And it was Tataw's soul that I was praying for so hard.

In the meantime, by the sovereignty of God, our church started broadcasting our services on television. My mother-in-law started to get up and watch on Sunday mornings, and I think that made Tataw curious. He knew what a smart lady he was married to, so our pastor, Ruffin Snow, must have something worthwhile to say if she was going to get up early to watch. He began to watch the services, too, and little by little, he saw in Pastor Ruffin a genuine man of God. God was creating a hunger in Tataw's heart and preparing him for his appointed time to meet, not only Ruffin, but The Master. I started praying for an "open door" for Pastor Ruffin to come talk to him.

One day, after visiting with Tataw, I was leaving when he got up and followed me to the door. To my great surprise, he handed me an Oklahoma University hat and asked me to give it to Ruffin. I knew that God had just provided the open door.

A little background to explain: Pastor Ruffin had moved to Hickory, North Carolina from Oklahoma, and he was a big sports fan. Tataw had learned about this from listening to Ruffin's sermons on television. Now, a long time ago, God in His wisdom had already given Tataw a golf buddy whose son just happened to be a coach for Oklahoma

University. Tataw asked "Whip" (his friend's nickname) to bring him a hat from OU. I never asked Tataw about it, but I always thought the hat was his way of reaching out to Christ through Ruffin.

I gave the hat to Ruffin that Sunday morning and told him about Tataw, his cancer, my prayer for an open door, and my concern over his soul. Pastor Ruffin told me that he would go see him that week. The next Saturday, I was using Tataw's computer when Ruffin drove up. I had never seen a more beautiful sight than this man of God walking through the yard. I felt like I was in a movie, and I ought to be hearing background music because to me, "the Cavalry" was coming through that door to rescue my hero. The truth of the matter is that it wasn't *the* "Cavalry" but "Calvary" riding to the rescue! Relief flooded over me.

My dear pastor visited Tataw several times and told him that he would be his pastor until he was well enough to be back to church. I think we all knew that, barring a miracle, he would not recover. On Ruffin's last visit, Tataw prayed and invited Christ into his heart!

God knows how each of us is made and He allowed Tataw to be ministered to by a man for whom he had utmost respect. Pastor Ruffin came in a gentle way that preserved Tataw's dignity and led him into his Savior's waiting arms.

THE BUTTERFLY STORY

The "butterfly" in this story is actually a dear friend of mine, Holly Wilcox. It is a story of triumph, tragedy, failure, redemption, life, and finally death. Well, maybe not so "finally" . . . .

Holly lived in my neighborhood with her mother, Mae. The reason I first noticed Holly was because she walked every day, like lots of other folks in this neighborhood, but what made Holly so noticeable was the **way** she walked: face forward, arms swinging vigorously, looking straight ahead as if so say, "Please don't talk to me or try to get to know me because if I slow down, I will have to face the truth, and I don't want to face the truth." You see, it was painfully obvious that Holly was anorexic.

Anyone could have recognized it by looking, but it really touched home with me because my sister had worn that same gaunt and empty look, years before. I watched my sister go from one of the most beautiful women on the planet to a skeleton as she battled anorexia and bulimia. I also watched God save her soul and deliver her completely and instantaneously. I knew that anorexia was no match for God. My sister was a miracle and I wanted to see a miracle happen to Holly. Sometimes God takes a long time to deliver and sometimes it happens immediately. He does things His way and His way is best.

I started to pray for Holly as I would see her pass by my house several times a day—every day. I would also pray with my children as we would kneel each night. When someone would say something about Holly and her condition, my little Becca, who was probably about five at the time, would confidently say, "My mommy is going to help her." She had no doubt that God would answer our cry for Holly. Oh, that we could all have—and keep—the faith of a little child!

Time went by and I was asked to help lead a Bible study at my church called "Breaking Free." I thought that if anyone needed to "break free," it was Holly. I told God that I would invite her to come the next time I saw her walk by. But each time I saw her, I would lose my nerve and put if off another day. I was afraid. What if she got mad? She didn't seem like she wanted to be bothered and after all, I barely knew her. Those thoughts would just swirl around in my mind, but finally I decided to say "No" to my fear and "Yes" to God, leaving both the questions and the consequences to Him.

So the next time Holly walked by, I took a deep breath and headed out the door, book in hand. I saw that determined look on her face as I raced across the yard. I called out, with heart beating wilding, "Holly!" She turned and all the hardness in her face melted into a beautiful smile. She looked like a walking skeleton, but nothing dimmed her smile and the sweet heart that was behind it.

I started talking to her about the Bible study, and to my great surprise, she told me that she had seen an announcement about the study in Sunday's paper and was very interested in attending. But since she didn't know anybody at that church, she thought that it might not be the right time for her.

Wow! I had no idea an announcement was even in Sunday's paper. All that time I was stalling, God was working it out to be the perfect time. I still haven't figured out how He does that. "Trust in the Lord with all your heart and lean not on your own understanding, in all your ways acknowledge Him, and He **will** make your paths straight" (Proverbs 3:5-6). I was beginning to see how true God's Word was—and is.

Holly was so excited to find out that she, indeed, did know someone at the church and that she had a personal invitation to attend, that she brought her mom to meet me to find out if she could come, too. Of course she could!

As we studied the Word each week, Holly became more and more uncomfortable. This study just hit too close to home for her. Before we could finish the study, she went into a treatment facility for her anorexia. While there, Holly was a model patient, but as soon as she got home, the old habits came back with a vengeance.

At one point, while her mother was out of town for a couple of weeks, I noticed that Holly's exercising became even more out of control. Without her mother, Holly had no boundaries, so she quickly started on a terrible downward spiral. Another member of the Bible study group even called after seeing Holly in a grocery store, telling me that somebody had to do something. I guessed that "somebody" had to be me.

I went to a neighbor's house and asked her to watch my kids for a few minutes and to pray because I was going to confront Holly about her anorexia. I walked to Holly's house and knocked on the door. She opened it, and I began to cry. I said that she probably knew why I was there, but to my amazement, she said she had no idea. When Holly looked into a mirror, she simply didn't see what the rest of us saw.

She invited me in, and I poured out my heart to her. I told her that I felt like I was watching somebody slowly kill themselves. I was crying like a baby, but while Holly was so tender and sweet, I noticed that she wasn't crying at all. Anorexia not only kills your body, it steals your humanity. It consumes you to the point of being unable to be in touch with normal human emotions. I finally just asked her how I could help her, and her only reply was that I could be her friend. I told her that I could—and would—definitely do that.

I came home feeling a little silly about how much I had blubbered. The reality was I barely even knew Holly, so I asked God if all of this was even any of my business. I opened my Bible to go back over what I had read in my quiet time that morning. I was in the book of Matthew 25:34-36 and it read: "Then the King will say to those on His right, 'Come, you who are blessed by My Father; take your inheritance, the kingdom prepared for you since the creation of the world. For I was **hungry** and you gave Me something to eat, I was a **stranger** and you invited Me in, I was in **prison** and you came to visit me'." Immediately it struck me that all of these things were true for Holly, either literally or figuratively—she had to be hungry, she had become a stranger to those who loved her, she was clothing her innermost self in hurtful ways, she was definitely sick, and she was being held captive in a mental prison.

I resumed reading.

> "Then the righteous will answer Him, 'Lord, when did we see You hungry and feed You, or thirsty and give You something to drink? When did we see You as a stranger and invite You in, or needing clothes and clothe You? When did we see You sick or in prison and go to visit You?' The King will reply, 'I tell you the truth, whatever you did for the least of these brothers (or sisters) of Mine, you did for Me.'"

When I read those words, I knew that they were meant to reassure me that I was in the center of God's will regarding Holly. What a thrill to hear from the King!

I started to go on walks with Holly and really got to know her. She was so interesting. She had a Master's Degree, had been a star athlete in school, and was a classic over-achiever in every way. We openly discussed her struggle with food and I was glad that she felt safe enough with me to "let me in." As time passed, I felt like I needed to ask her about her salvation and if she really knew Jesus as savior. She told me that she did, and I felt a huge relief because the truth was that I was afraid that she could die any day.

Holly tried hard to get out of the pit that she was living in, but she was absolutely powerless over the hold it had on her. Her precious mother, Mae, was so supportive and kind. She was the kind of mother that all kids dream of having. But there came a point when Mae had to make one of the hardest decisions that a mother could ever make. She went to the magistrate and had Holly forcibly taken into treatment. She was devastated and so was Holly. I admire Mae so much for putting her relationship with Holly on the line in order to save her life. Some parents don't have the guts to take such a step. Mae is one tough lady as far as I'm concerned!

Holly was sent to a treatment center in Tallahassee, Florida, and she was away for several months. I prayed for her and wrote to her, and she responded with the sweetest note to me.

Around Christmas, Holly and Mae came by the house to visit and bring me some cookies. I hadn't laid eyes on Holly since she had gone to the treatment center in Florida, and when I saw her, I screamed! She was well! She was beautiful and showed no signs of anorexia, inside or out. She was just fit, trim, and lovely. I remember staring at her hands because they no longer looked like the hands of a skeleton. Just as importantly, they were folded in her lap. Now it may sound strange that I noticed something like that, but it told me that she was actually relaxed and not on guard like she used to be. She felt comfortable in her body and was no longer a prisoner in it. She had indeed "broken free."

A few months passed, and Holly was doing great. She had a job, was journaling and reading her Bible daily for direction. She prayed about everything and was so happy. I felt as though Holly was like Lazarus in the Bible—this was a resurrection.

One day my phone rang, and when I picked it up, Holly was on the other end, frantic. She was so upset because she had accidentally run over a neighbor's cat. Mae told me later that she cried and cried over that little animal. Another miracle—Holly had even found her tears. God had brought her full circle.

A few weeks later, I came home from teaching an exercise class. My mother-in-law gave me such a serious look that I knew something wasn't right. She asked, "Have you heard about Holly?" When I told her that I hadn't and asked what was wrong, she told me that a neighbor had called and told her that Holly had died the day before in a car accident! I raced to Mae's house, and when she opened the door, all I could say was, "Is it true?"

She said that it was, and we just stood in the doorway and held onto each other. I felt like I was in a bad dream, and all I wanted was to wake up.

Mae called me before the funeral service and asked if I would speak at the funeral. I said that I would be honored, but that if I spoke about my relationship with Holly, I would have to talk about her anorexia. I wanted to know if that would be all right because the last thing I wanted to do was add to Mae's pain. But she said that talking about Holly's anorexia would be telling the truth and I was free to share whatever I wanted to. I told you she was a tough lady.

I asked God to speak through me, giving me the word that would bring comfort to a very devastated family while, at the same time, bring truth to all in attendance. Jeremiah 32:27 says, "I am the Lord, the God of all mankind. Is anything too hard for Me?" What happened next just blew me away. Stick with me now and you'll see what I mean.

Mae had talked so much about Holly being her "butterfly" because of the incredible metamorphosis that had happened to her. So, as I was thinking about what to say at Holly's funeral, the thought of the butterfly kept rolling around in my head. I got out my World Book and looked up the life cycle of the butterfly. I was amazed at the parallels between the butterfly's life cycle and Holly's life, and I began making notes for the service.

The day of the funeral, my friend, Vickie Vaughan, picked me up to go to the church, and I got cold feet all of a sudden.

I had never spoken at a funeral and didn't exactly know the protocol, and I found myself thinking, *What have I done? I've just written down the life cycle of butterfly and I'm actually going to read it at a funeral.*

I looked at Vickie and said, "Could I read this to you and have you be honest with me and tell me if it sounds silly?" I read part of it and when I looked up, she had tears streaming down her face. I didn't want to start crying, too, so I stopped reading and decided that it must be just fine.

At the church, we had gotten seated when the preacher came up to me, asking if I was Terri. I said that I was, and I showed her what I had prepared to say. She thought it was a little lengthy (she didn't read it, but I guess it just looked lengthy), and again I felt a little panicked. I wondered how I could shorten it, and I looked at Vickie, not knowing what to do. She thought I should go ahead with it just like it was. I wasn't so sure—until the preacher walked out of a side room with her robe on and the scarf draped around her neck was covered in butterflies! Vickie and I looked at each other in amazement. At that time, I wasn't used to God doing things like that in my life. But I was feeling better; God was obviously going to use what I had written down.

And then as the service was beginning, a multimedia presentation of Holly's life began to play on a screen at the front of the church. Holly's name came upon the screen **encased in a huge butterfly**. God's unseen hand had planned the whole service as one cohesive unit even though none of us had discussed what we were going to do beforehand.

When it came time for me to speak, I just shared with all the people what was in my heart, including much of what you've already read in this story. I'm not one to write down what I'm going to say verbatim, but I since I was quoting from an encyclopedia, I did write down the second half of my talk. How thankful I am that I actually kept it and am able to record it here:

> *"As we all witnessed, Holly did overcome her fear and give all to her Savior. We watched as the Author of Life, the Lord Jesus, brought her out of that cocoon and how she was transformed into a beautiful butterfly. That's how Mae described what happened to Holly: 'She was like a butterfly.'*
>
> *"I don't pretend to understand why Holly was taken away from us after overcoming so much. Mae talked so much about her 'little butterfly' that I thought I would research a little about the life cycle of the butterfly and see if there were a few parallels for us.*
>
> *"The egg stage sometimes lasts months. The larva stage lasts at least two weeks. The pupa (cocoon) lasts from a few days to more than a year. The adult (actual butterfly) lasts only one or two weeks. In World Book, it reads, 'The butterfly is one of the most beautiful of all insects. People have always been charmed by the delicate, gorgeously colored wings of butterflies. The beauty and grace of these insects have inspired artists and poets.'*
>
> *"When I see a butterfly, I'm blown away by its beauty and I'm in awe of its Creator. That was how I felt when Holly came to see me after Christmas. I was amazed by the metamorphosis that had taken place, body and soul. She was beautiful, and the sparkle in her brown eyes brought tears of joy to mine. I was blown away by <u>her</u> beauty and in awe of <u>her</u> Creator. Truly a miracle sat before me.*
>
> *We all prayed for Holly's recovery. God heard, and in His love and mercy, He answered. Like the butterfly, our time with her seemed far too short. But no one can take away those weeks that we all got to spend with Holly, so well and full of life. Indeed, her last days were a gift to all of us who knew and loved her. I know that when I got the terrible news on Monday morning about Holly's death, I felt as though all the air was taken from my lungs. After all that she went through, why? I don't have the answer. I just know that the value of our lives is not measured by how many years we spend on this earth.*
>
> *Think for a moment with me about the most precious feet that ever touched the soil of this planet. His name was Jesus of Nazareth. His life only lasted 33 years. Upon His death, His friends felt*

totally confused and helpless. If only they could have peeled away the natural world and seen the spiritual, they would have realized that the greatest victory in the world had just taken place.

Revelation 1:17 says, 'Do not be afraid. I am the first and the last. I am the Living One; I was dead, and behold I am alive forever and ever! And I hold the keys to death and hades.' God's plan was complete for Holly but we, like Jesus' friends, are left stunned and devastated. I love those words from Revelation, and many times they have been my comfort, like the words found in Isaiah 55:8-9, which say, 'My thoughts are not your thoughts, neither are your ways My ways,' declares the Lord. 'As the heavens are higher than your ways and My thoughts than your thoughts.'

To close my remarks, I chose the words of Paul found in II Timothy, and I believe they could also be Holly's words to us, . . . and the time has come for my departure. I have fought the good fight, I have finished the race, I have kept the faith. Now there is in store for me the crown of righteousness, which the Lord, the righteous Judge, will award to me on that day—not only to me, but also to all who have longed for His appearing."

Holly won the only race that mattered in the end—the race of faith.

Tataw's Story: The Song

This story is so tender and wonderful that I hope it will give all readers a little insight into the unsearchable sweetness of God.

As you read previously in "The Hat Story", Tataw was diagnosed with bladder cancer in 1998. We were all just brokenhearted with the news. Tataw loved life and adored his family. He never wanted to miss a single moment of any of our lives. When my children were involved in sports, he not only came to the games, he went to the practices. When he came to their games, he filmed every play. Now keep in mind that the kids were so young that they just grouped together and fought over the ball, which meant that watching one of their games was actually more like observing an amoeba migrating across the floor than it was watching a real basketball game. It was hilarious. The best part was getting back home to a big lunch that Memaw had prepared and then sitting down to watch every play—again. I think the only person who enjoyed watching those games twice was Tataw.

My oldest son, Andrew, started taking guitar lessons when he was eleven years old. True to form, Tataw wanted to hear every new thing that he learned and be involved in every part of his new venture. If Andrew went to the back of the house to practice in private, Tataw would sneak back there and stand outside the door just to listen.

Andrew became obsessed with that guitar and played all the time (he is now twenty-three years old and is a worship leader). Tataw beamed with pride as he watched Andrew learn and improve, bragging to anyone who would listen. But when cancer struck Tataw, he grew weaker and weaker, even as Andrew's talent grew stronger and stronger. In 2002, Andrew made a tape of himself playing the guitar and gave it to Tataw as a gift. Often, when I would pop in for a visit, I would find him lying there, eyes closed, just soaking in Andrew's music.

Time marched on and we all watched Tataw as cancer ravaged his body. This man had always taken care of everything for all of us, cleaning house, working in the yard for hours, playing golf twice a week, staying active in so many ways, but now he had become someone who couldn't even get off the couch by himself. It was so hard for him and just as hard for all of us to watch. Please understand—we loved taking care of him, and it was never a burden. But it was just hard for him to receive after being such a giver all of his life. God's Word says we "reap what we sow." This was certainly true for Tataw, who was a sower of "giving and loving", and when he needed "giving and loving," he reaped a mighty harvest.

My mother-in-law silently preached to me some of the greatest sermons I ever heard as I watched her care for her husband of nearly fifty years. I never once heard her complain or treat him in any other way than pure love. She wouldn't leave his side except to get her hair done or go to the store once a week. She completely gave her life and every ounce of energy to him. When he would fall and call for her, she would come get him up and make light of the whole thing. Then I would see her go to the back of the house and cry over his pain and the loss of his dignity. She didn't know that we saw her at those times, but we saw, and we knew. I hope to grow up some day and be like Memaw.

Andrew started playing guitar for the youth at our church. We would tell Tataw about it, and I knew that he longed to be there with us, to hear and see it for himself. He would tell me that when he got stronger, he was coming to watch Andrew play. In my heart, I knew that day would never come.

One weekend, my mother came to visit and she got to see Andrew play, and she was so excited that she was talking a mile a minute when we got to Tataw's house after church. He looked up at me and asked if Andrew had played in church that morning. By this time, our church services were broadcast on television and Memaw and Tataw could get up and watch each Sunday. I liked to think of them as "virtual members" of our church. As soon as Tataw asked me that question, I knew why. He wanted so badly to see Andrew perform, and he knew if Andrew played in the church service it would be broadcast on television, he would be able to see and hear it for himself. Well, that just made my heart melt, and immediately, I determined in my mind to come up with a plan to get Andrew on television before our sweet Tataw died. I thought to myself, *"Maybe I could call the choir director and explain what the situation is and he'll let Andrew play something."* Sounds easy, right? But I knew it would put the choir director in an impossible situation. Andrew was only thirteen and hadn't been playing guitar for that long. We go to a huge church that has one of the best choirs and orchestras in the entire state. Who was I to say that my son was good enough to play solo with a singer during a Sunday morning service?

I quickly dismissed that idea and went on to another one. I remembered that a man from church, Mike Roberts, had sung a song with just a guitar accompaniment years before. I contemplated asking him to choose a song and let Andrew play. Another look at that wasted little body on the couch reminded me just how close to death Tataw was, and I nearly despaired of being able to work anything out in time.

I got in my car to go pick up pizza for everyone and in desperation looked up to God and told Him that I couldn't work this thing out. It was just too impossible for me. I asked Him to work it out for me if He would. I knew from previous experience that nothing was too hard for my God. But with all that was going on in this big world, would He look down and care enough about my problem to hear my small cry for a man who meant so much to me? I got reassurance as I remembered the words from Ephesians 3:20: "Now to Him who is able to do exceedingly, abundantly above all we think or ask . . . ."

That was Sunday afternoon. At about 11:00 on the following Monday morning, the phone rang. It was Mike Roberts! As he started to leave a message, I grabbed the phone and said "Hello."

He proceeded to ask me if we were going to be in town July 20 because he wanted Andrew to play the guitar for him!

Stunned at this turn of events, I said, "Mike, I just asked God yesterday to have you call me. I wanted you to sing a song and let Andrew play because his grandfather is dying of cancer."

Mike replied, "That gives me chills."

Now my husband (who didn't know I had even prayed this prayer) was sitting on the couch reading the paper and listening to my side of this conversation. I watched the paper gently collapse onto his face and his whole body started to shake uncontrollably as tears streamed down his sweet face. My living room was suddenly transformed into Holy Ground! What a mighty God we serve!

When we got together with Mike, he shared with us that he had already picked out a song before he knew anything about Tataw. It was called "Home." The words were so incredible and so perfect for him. They talked of "Home" as being where our history would begin, of where we would dance with Jesus. In a sense, the words literally rolled out the red carpet and welcomed Tataw into the presence of God.

The big day finally came and none too soon. In fact, I told one of the men in charge that Tataw probably wouldn't be alive by the time it aired the next Sunday. They assured me that they would get me a copy as soon as the service was over.

Mike made his way to the microphone, and Andrew stepped out and went up to the platform. My mother burst into tears, while I felt as if I would burst as I sat there just basking in the goodness of God. Mike proceeded to tell the whole story of the situation—the cancer, the prayer, the song, the chills—and he said, "All I can say to you, Tataw, is how much the Father must love you." Then he said, "I'm glad we serve a God that cares about our dreams because Tataw always wanted to see Andrew play guitar on TV. Today that dream is going to come true."

Andrew started to play, and he played beautifully and flawlessly. (I know I'm a little biased but he did!). I don't think there was a dry eye in the place. That worship service was the sweetest service that I have ever been a part of. After the song, we had communion and remembered what it cost for such a great salvation—the blood and broken body of Jesus. God's presence was there in a palpable way.

I raced home with the video. When I walked in the door, I warned Memaw that in the film, Mike stated that Andrew's grandfather was dying. You see, although it was obvious to all of us, we had never discussed this with Tataw. Until the very end, he held onto the hope that he would get better, and we allowed that hope to live.

We previewed the tape (as much as we could see through the streaming tears), and Memaw said, "I think he needs to see the whole thing."

We woke Tataw and told him that we had the song. Memaw reached through the bars on his hospital bed and held tightly to his hand, putting a box of tissues between them. The rest of us just gathered in that tiny room, surrounding that man that we loved so much, letting God minister to him through that song. The tears flowed. Tataw was such a private and strong man, not given to showing his emotions outwardly. But in that moment, those walls just crumbled, and he loved openly with everything in him. I think that was the first time I had ever seen him cry like that—unashamedly and freely. What a precious time. At the end of the song, he looked at Andrew, held up his rail-thin arms, Andrew came to him, and they held each other. No words were needed.

After everyone else had left the room, he said to me, "You don't know how hard I had to fight to stay alive last night to be here for this."

Through tears I said, "You don't have to fight anymore, Tataw. You don't have to be afraid—you can go home."

He said, "I'm not afraid. God is with me."

Later, when everyone returned to the room, he said to all of us, "I want to plan my funeral." Mike's words had given him permission to talk about his death with all of us. We planned what he wanted. Of course he wanted Andrew to play the guitar and he wanted Matt, his granddaughter's husband, to sing.

Six days later—the day before the broadcast of the song on television—Tataw went "Home."

THE "F" WORD STORY

The greatest privilege I have ever known is being called daughter by my Heavenly Father. I get up every morning, and I crack open His love letters to me (aka The Bible) and I experience intimacy with my Creator and Redeemer. Through those letters, I realize how important I am to Him, and I've learned that anything that bothers me is something that He wants to talk about, deal with, and put behind us. He will either show me where I've been wrong, or speak to me about the other person (and then have me pray about what He shows me about the person or the situation), or comfort my heart and let me know that He understands and that He'll handle it. There are limitless ways He will speak to my heart because He is my Shepherd, and I hear and know His voice. Oh, that all of His children would start to plumb the depths of God's richness! A relationship with Him is so much more than keeping the rules.

I have also found that nothing slips by Him and nothing is insignificant; if it hurts me, it touches His heart because He cares so deeply for me. It doesn't matter why I'm upset; it could be something I brought on myself, something done to me to by someone else, or just life, in general. My Lord always wants my conscience clear and my heart open to Him so that His Living Water is free to flow all day.

I'm so glad I've learned through the years that it's not my sin that will keep me away from Him; it's my stiffness. I once heard Steve Brown say that you can hug a dirty child, but you can't hug a stiff child. I've found that many people are so concerned about not ever sinning that they completely miss any joy and love in their relationship with God. God hates sin because it creates a fog that keeps me from seeing

Him and His glorious face as it really is. Seen through that fog, His presence will scare me instead of comfort me.

That's the way I feel about my children. I never want anything between us—not because I want perfect children (there's no such thing), or because I want some kind of total control over them, but because I love them so much, I never want my presence to scare them. Every child knows this feeling; you've done something wrong, your parents walk in the door, and immediately your heart begins to pound and you're looking for someplace to hide. You still love your parents, but they no longer seem warm and comforting to you; in your mind, parent has been replaced by "judge." It's not that they've suddenly changed; it's just that your guilty conscience has fogged up their face.

I want to be a safe place that my children always run to for comfort and help, even if they've done something terrible. What a burden children carry when they have to shoulder a parent's fragile ego! I think one of the most horrible things a parent can say is, "What are the neighbors/people going to think?" Inadvertently, a parent is telling a child, "All that matters is what people think, not what God knows."

We teach children early on to be good little hypocrites. We also teach them about God whether we choose to or not. The way we treat our children will greatly determine the way they think about God. I decided early on in my little ones' lives that I was going to do everything in my power to be "one" with God so that He could parent through me. In chapter seventeen of the book of John, Jesus prayed that you and I would be one with Him just like He and the Father are one. Whoa! That means it's possible to truly be one with God because that's what Jesus prayed. I take Him at His Word. You see, He always knows what's wrong with my kids (even when I don't), why they feel the way they do (even when they don't), and He will always have answers and help for us. My responsibility is to stay connected "at the source." Remember—Jesus told the woman at the well that, even with all of her sins, she could **ask** and **have** Living Water. We are no exception. Jesus died an excruciating and horrible death so that His very Spirit could live in these bodies—**our** bodies. Don't settle for anything less!

My favorite evangelist, Bill Stafford, often says during his sermons, "You've got as much of God as you want." That used to sound so harsh to me, but now I look at that statement, and I think it's full of hope. The ball is in my court. I'm not a victim of my past, my circumstances, or anything else. I can go directly to God, and He can come to me and fill me with His presence if I'm willing to wholeheartedly give myself to Him.

I have a perfect and sweet example of "Him through me" with my middle son, Scott. One night when he was ten years old, I walked into his bedroom and could just sense that something wasn't right. I started to question him and, as I did, he got very upset. I never let things like that go, so I settled in and started asking questions: "Did someone say or do something to you? Did you say or do something wrong?" Well, he proceeded to start pouring out everything he could remember ever having done wrong. Being only ten and homeschooled, you can imagine what his little offenses would consist of. He told me that he went to a neighbor's house and since the parents weren't home, the daughter told him he didn't have to take his shoes off, so he didn't. His conscience bothered him immediately, so he went back to the door and took his shoes off. I know it may sound silly, but from the time the kids were little, I always wanted complete honesty. I had been such a little liar, and I know from experience that a little liar turns into a big liar. As I listened to my little precious boy pour out his heart, I was just devastated inside that his little heart and conscience had been hurting so badly, and I didn't know it.

Scott has always had a very tender conscience, and without an understanding of God's grace, it probably would have driven the little fellow crazy. He even told me to quit telling people all the time how wonderful he was, because in his mind, he wasn't.

Our talking back and forth went on for an hour or more. At that point, I honestly could have cared less what he had done—I just wanted him to have relief. Out of the blue I blurted out, "Scott, I don't care if you said the 'F' word! I would gladly forgive you. I love you and nothing will ever change that. The **only** reason that I'm even trying to get you to tell me is because I want to give you my forgiveness." I was desperate for him to truly feel relief.

I told him that I had felt really badly about some things in my past, things I had confessed to Rick, my husband and Scott's daddy. I told him that Rick had told me that I didn't have to confess everything because the past was the past, and he forgave me for anything and everything. That idea seemed to appeal to Scott, and he said that he felt better. I had my doubts, but I hugged him and went out with my heart still heavy because I could tell total relief was not there.

A few days later, I could tell that Scott felt all heavy and sad again. I asked him to come into the bedroom and let me talk to him. He started to cry and I begged him to tell me what was wrong. I assured him over and over again that I didn't care what he had done—I just wanted to know so that we could put it behind us. We probably talked for an hour or more, and each time it seemed he'd built up enough courage to tell me "the big sin," he would bury his face in the pillow and say, "I can't."

Eventually, Scott realized that I wasn't going anywhere until this was out in the open, so he faced his worst fear and told me all about it.

Scott had gone to the skatepark to ride his skateboard, and while he was there, he heard the "F" word for the first time in his life. He told me that the word just rolled around in his head, and he started saying rhyming words that got close to it, but he didn't actually say it. And then one day as he was doing that, he accidentally said the "F" word. He had felt guilty for months.

I took my little lamb in my arms and said, "Who knew that you said that but God?"

Scott sniffed out, "Nobody."

Now remember that just a few days earlier, I'd actually brought up the possibility that saying that dreaded word was the problem! I said, "God spoke those words through your mommy because He wanted you to feel better and not be afraid or feel guilty anymore. There are six billion people on this planet, and God saw that there was a ten-year-old little boy in this house that was in misery and He couldn't stand it. I had absolutely no way of knowing what you did. That's just how much He loves you!"

We cried and hugged, and God's Spirit was in that room with us in a way that I really can't even put into words. My little Scott felt not only special but clean and forgiven.

As I was typing this story, he walked into the kitchen, and we started talking about it. After we had a good laugh (he's 19 now), he told me that this very incident was a big turning point for him in understanding God's grace.

"He tends His flock like a shepherd; He gathers the lambs in His arms and carries them close to His heart; He gently leads those that have young" (Isaiah 40:11).

Need He say more?

The Christmas Story

This particular story is part of this book because my precious sister, Robin Ringley, reminded me of it as I was trying to remember all the different stories that I wanted to include. She even remembered the scripture references although it happened many years ago. It is my Christmas Story and one of my children still remembers this as the best Christmas that we ever had. This story was so pivotal for me because it was a time when I decided to trust God and it looked like He was going to let me sink, but He didn't: He took me to a new level of trust. I'm so glad He did because He knew how much I was going to need Him as He continued to take me deeper. You will read about it in "My Most Painful Story" near the end of this book. Don't jump ahead; enjoy the journey.

I've found out that each of us is on our own personal journey, but God lets our lives affect all of those around us. Our lives will either tell them that there is a God in heaven who is completely trustworthy or that we are on our own and we better scrape and fight for all we can while we're down here. Or as a good Baptist preacher would say, "Get all you can, can what you get and then sit on the can!" I decided years ago that since I didn't have a mentor of my own that really took God at His word and lived a life of faith, that I would be that person by God's grace and try to help my family and friends believe God. A great Christian once said that he was clearing a path so others following wouldn't have to struggle as he did. I said all of that to say that the reason Robin remembers this story so vividly is because she has watched me through the years and has hopefully found it easier to believe God because she has seen Him rescue me over and over again. In this case, He used her and her generous husband to be my deliverers. Only God knows how much I love and appreciate her and her family. I often tell her that I feel sorry for all the women in the world that don't get to have her for a sister because I got the best!

I can't remember the exact year this all happened but it was probably around 2003. I was trying with all of my heart to believe God and live by faith, but as you see from several stories, I have not been blessed with lots of money. I'm glad God says that my faith is more precious than gold because I don't have gold, silver, or even much paper money. I am only wealthy in one area and that's faith. I strive with all my heart to be the equivalent of a billionaire (faithfully speaking) and to give generously to anyone in need.

This particular Christmas was after I had surrendered everything to God and I not only wanted Him be glorified through our Christmas, I wanted to trust Him more. I talked to the kids and told them that Jesus only got three gifts from the wise men, so they could choose three gifts and I would spend about a hundred dollars on each. I didn't have three hundred dollars, but I decided that I would sell my wedding ring instead of using a credit card. I wear the band but not my diamond, so I assured my sweet Rick that I didn't mind having to sell it. Although it broke my heart on one hand, what it really hurt was my pride. I had never been so desperate that I sold jewelry. I went into a local jewelry store and the person I talked to told me that she would give me two hundred dollars. I was shocked. It cost Rick $1800.00 (and that was when $1800.00 was a lot of money) and I couldn't believe all I would get was $200! I left so I could think about whether I really wanted to do this or not.

As Christmas was approaching, I left one morning to teach an exercise class and decided that I would go ahead and do it. Part of my daily reading was 2 Kings 18:13-37 that day. It described a time in Hezekiah's life when an enemy (Sennacherib, king of Assyria) had come against Judah. In fear, Hezekiah paid him off by taking all the silver that was found in the temple of the LORD and the treasuries of the royal palace. He even stripped off the gold that covered the doors and doorposts and gave it to Sennacherib. The unfortunate part of the story was that using gold instead of trusting God got Hezekiah nowhere. The king of Assyria kept advancing and was trying to take possession of Judah, and with his mighty army, it looked like he would. Then as I read on in chapters 18 and then 19, I saw how Hezekiah finally, with no other place to turn, took these written threats from this king, went to the temple of the LORD and spread the letters out before Him. He said, "O LORD, God of Israel, enthroned between the cherubim, you alone are God over all the kingdoms of the earth. You have made heaven and earth. Give ear, O LORD, and hear; open your eyes, O LORD, and see; listen to the word Sennacherib has sent to insult the Living God." In verse 19, I saw what God loved most about Hezekiah's prayer. He said, "Now, O LORD our God, deliver us from his hand, **so that** all kingdoms on earth may **know** that you alone, O LORD, are God." Hezekiah asked for deliverance **so that** the glory of God would be obvious and people would be drawn to Him. That's what I started to ask God. I asked Him to show Himself to and through me so that all those I loved would know He was real. I especially wanted Robin to believe God with all of her heart. Religion had done so much damage to both of us growing up that we came into Christianity with so much baggage and distorted beliefs about what God was like. I not only wanted to be free from it, I wanted to help carry her to freedom with me.

After Hezekiah prayed that prayer, an angel of the LORD put to death a hundred and eighty-five thousand men in Assyria. Wow! That's power! I couldn't believe how God responded to that prayer of faith. After this reading, I felt like God was saying that He wanted to deliver me and that He didn't want me trusting in silver or gold like Hezekiah had done. My wedding ring was given to me by my sweet husband and it represented more than just money; it was a symbol of our covenant. I wanted to believe that, but I also knew that my pride definitely did not want to walk back in that jewelry store. Anytime I feel my pride popping up, I doubt whether I'm hearing from God because I can't trust myself. I was in the jewelry store's parking lot preparing to go in and was near tears because life was just so hard that I felt faithless, tired and humiliated. It's one thing to sit in my house and read all about this all-powerful God, but quite another thing to be in the reality of being broke and feeling like I could be delusional with all my faith talk. I was sitting in the parking lot of the jewelry store and I decided to just get out and get it over with. I opened the door and stepped out of my car, but it started to snow so hard and fast that I thought that if I didn't get home quickly, I might not make it home. I thought to myself, "Is this how God is stopping me from selling my ring?" Wouldn't the people in the parking lot have laughed if they had known that I thought that snow storm just might have been sent for me?

I got in my car and drove home. At about eleven o'clock that morning, I called my sister to chat. I had told her absolutely nothing about anything that was going on with me concerning all of this. After a little small talk, she proceeded to tell me that she had put a check in the mail for me for $300.00! I then told her, as Paul Harvey would say, "The rest of the story."

⋆ ⋆ ⋆

As an addendum to this story, I just have to share what my sister told me when I called and read this story to her. She said the night before she sent me the money, she and her husband were sitting in their living room watching television. She was sitting there thinking about me and my family and feeling like we might need help with Christmas (now remember—I had shared nothing about my situation with her). She hadn't discussed this with Hank at all. She said as she was thinking, Hank looked at her and said, "Write a check for three hundred dollars and send it to Terri."

Robin then reminded me that when I called her the next day, I opened up my prayer journal and read to her about talking to God that very morning about what to do, the ring, my daily Bible reading, all of it.

This made me want to find that prayer journal from all those years ago, so I went to our storage building and dug around until I found all my old prayer journals. After looking through several (since I wasn't sure about the date), I found the one I was looking for and found that the date was actually December 9, 2002. The entry I made that day was about our phone call.

It said:

> *"I called Robin this morning to tell her the power was on (there had been a power outage due to snow I think). Out of the blue she told*

me that she sent $300 this morning; the exact amount that I asked for. You did deliver me without me having to sell my ring. Praise You for Your deliverance. Praise You for letting me and Rick together experience this. You're so wonderful."

And He is even more wonderful to me now!

The Name

". . . for You have exalted above ALL things
Your Name and Your Word."
(Psalm 138:2)

This story started to develop on July 4, 2010. My boys and I were at Wal-Mart, and they wanted a movie to watch that night. So off we trotted to The Redbox to start the arduous task of finding a movie that I would watch. It's hard these days because it has to pass my church lady test. I love to spend time with my family, so when they told me that a certain movie was awesome with only a little language, I reluctantly agreed. I wasn't sure where the line was drawn for me about language because it's normally not an issue for me. I'm usually cooking, cleaning, or reading. Well, there is my daily walk on the wild side—every night at 7:00, I sit down to watch Jeopardy. No wonder God had me call this book, "The Ordinary Road."

We sat down to watch the movie, and I warned everyone that if it was bad, I was leaving. Well, the movie was great. It was a psychological thriller with a great plot and no sexual content. As I was watching, completely engrossed, one of the characters said "g**d***" (I hate even typing that much). I felt like a knife pierced my soul. I thought about leaving, but I thought maybe it was the only time it would be used. Well, it wasn't. I heard it several more times, and since I had sat through it once, the second time got easier and then, although I hated hearing it, I tried to just block it out and pay attention to the movie.

After the movie, I went into the living room and thought, "What did I just do?" I felt terrible. I hadn't watched a movie with language like that since I had become a Christian twenty-two years ago. I try to sort through my own guilt and true Holy Spirit conviction; there is a difference, and sometimes I have to hear directly from Him before I know. One thing I am sure of as God's child is that I have the privilege of a face-to-face relationship. I can carry everything to Him, and He will not only tell me the truth—He is The Truth.

I'll record my journal entry that next morning:

> *"Please speak, Lord* (I always start my journaling that way), *I feel like my Scott did after he said the 'F' word. Please come, my Father, and hold me and let me know that our relationship is okay. I have a new line drawn, and I never want to watch something like that again. I got my belly full. It doesn't even appeal to me. I have no excuse. I'm devastated, and I wish I was better. I'm sorry. I can't take having Your back to me. Again, help me sort through emotions to truth."*

I am putting down what my feelings were as I talked to God. I know His back was not toward me, but I felt that way. Feelings lie to us, but my prayer journal recordings are my heart, not perfect theology. They are a child's cry to her Father. When we sin, our first response is to run and not face God. We turn our backs, God doesn't turn His.

I started reading my Bible, and I will record the scriptures I read that morning:

"David again brought together out of Israel chosen men, thirty thousand in all. He and all his men set out from Baalah of Judah to bring up from there the ark of God, which is called by **Name**, the name of The Lord Almighty who is enthroned between the cherubim that are on the ark." (Second Samuel 6:1-2)

When I read those words, my living room was suddenly transformed into Holy ground. When I saw the Name with that capital "N" and how seriously God took His Name, I wanted to just die. I also knew the rest of that story about the ark: Uzzah reached out to steady it, and God killed Him. God was showing David and all those people how Holy He is and how He is to be respected. The ark was not to be touched because it was the place where the glory of God rested, between the cherubim. That's why the Israelites were commanded to carry it only with poles through the rings on the four corners of it. Uzzah reached out to steady it because it was being carried on a cart pulled by oxen instead of the prescribed way that God told them to in His law. David knew better, but had somehow thought that he could get away with doing things his way. What a sobering reminder about the "otherness" of God Almighty. If it weren't for the blood of Jesus, God would have to kill us all in His Holy presence. Sometimes, we all forget just who this God is that we so flippantly approach.

I'll continue with my journal entry made after reading the rest of that chapter in Second Samuel:

> *"Uzzah is what I'm reading about; You struck him dead because of his irreverence. To listen to Your Name as a byword is unforgivable. You would have been justified in striking me dead. I'm so, so, so very sorry for dishonoring You and dishonoring You in front of my family. I bring it to You with Jesus' precious blood as my only defense. Please wash it away (east from west) and use it for good. Please let it be an 'all things' (Roman's 8:28) in my life."*

I had to speak in Sunday School that morning, so as I was preparing, I told God that I would tell the whole class about this if He wanted me to. I found out a long time ago that God is not concerned about my reputation or protecting it; He is interested in truth. He didn't hide His saints' faults and sins. He put them in the Bible and they help me when I fail. The worst thing I can ever do is tell people only the good things I do and let them think I'm much more spiritual than I really am. That would be real failure. By the time I had met with God, been put in my place by Him, trembled at His Word, repented, and—Hallelujah!—been joyfully restored, I was anxious to go and share with the class all that had happened. Paul said that he would boast in his weaknesses so that the power of Christ would rest on him. I will gladly tell anyone how weak I am so that I can have my Christ; nothing compares to His presence and power.

I went to church and shared with my Sunday School class what had transpired since the night before. I cried some as I talked and some cried with me. Some probably thought I was crazy, and many probably think I'm a little over the edge. I would say I'm a lot over the edge, and that's where I want to be. I don't want to be careful and cautious; I want to live out loud and full throttle for my Jesus, with no compromise.

I know it sounds crazy, but when God gives me a boundary, instead of making me feel hemmed in and stifled, it makes me feel safe and loved.

Not long after this all happened and I was happy in my "gd" free world, a dear friend of mine brought me a book that she loved so much that she said she had to share it with me. She brought me a card with a big-haired lady on it (I have very thick, curly hair—what we in the South often refer to as "**big hair**," or as it is usually pronounced "**har**.") ; inside it read, "The higher the hair, the closer to God." She is one of the sweetest and funniest Christian friends I have. I won't name the book she bought for me, but I will tell you what she wrote inside the front cover, "To Terri, my dear friend and prayer warrior. From (her name)—With all the love and gratitude my 'beepy' heart can muster! In reading this book, I thought of you many times, but especially in the following: 'Rumor is you got some kind of power prayer, get better results than just the regular variety.' And ' . . . we all on a party line to God, but you (Terri), you sitting right in His ear.' I love you, (her name)."

Well, that nearly broke my heart and made me so grateful to have the honor of such a friend.

I started reading the book, and it was great. The story just sucked you right in and the characters were so real that you could just see them with your mind's eye. As I was enjoying it so much, all of a sudden I came upon the word g**d***. It hit me like a baseball bat. I wondered if it was ok to read on with that word. I was honestly not sure. I didn't want to insult my friend, but I knew I couldn't insult God. What was I to do? Is it okay to read it as long as I'm not hearing it? Where is my line now? I never expected to have a dilemma like this. I thought that maybe I could put in on Becca's Ipad and get all the bad words removed and not have to tell my friend that I couldn't read it. I'm human and I care deeply about making a decision that affects others and that may misrepresent God somehow. People feel guilty enough often without adding fuel to the fire. I couldn't find a way to get the words removed, so I asked God in my quiet time what I was to do.

My daily reading that day was in I Kings 13: "The Man of God From Judah." I'm going to paraphrase the story a bit. A man of God came from Judah to Bethel because God had told him to. He was to deliver a message to the king and then go back home a different way. He was also told not to eat bread or drink water, but to just head back home. A prophet met him along the way back and told the man of God that God had given him (the prophet) a different message for him. The prophet told him to come to his house and eat and drink. God had clearly already given him direction, but he foolishly listened to this prophet and went with him. I'll quote verses 16-21 of that chapter:

"The man of God said, 'I cannot turn back and go with you, nor can I eat bread or drink water with you in this place. I have been told by the word of the LORD: 'You must not eat bread or drink water there or return by the way you came'."

"The old prophet answered, 'I too am a prophet, as you are. And an angel said to me by the word of the LORD: 'Bring him back with you to your house so that he may eat bread and drink water' (But he was lying to him). So the man of God returned with him and ate and drank in his house."

"While they were sitting at the table, the word of the LORD came to the old prophet who had brought him back. He cried out to the man of God who had come from Judah, 'This is what the LORD says: 'You have **defied** the word of the LORD and have not kept the command the LORD your God gave you'."

As much as I could discern what God was saying to me, I gathered from this story that God had already given that man a command and to not keep it completely was to defy God. By the way, the prophet in that story was eaten by a lion. I've found that God is not always warm and fuzzy with us when it comes to our sin.

I told a friend about not being able to read this particular book. She loved the book (and me) so much that she offered graciously to take it home and mark out all the bad words. I didn't really know what to say or do at this offer. I didn't want to offend her either and wasn't sure (again) what God would want me to do. She had already read the book and didn't mind seeing that word to mark it out. I let her take it and bring it back, not really sure whether this was right either. When I got it back, I decided I would read it unless or until I saw that word even one time. If so, I would put it down for good. Well, I saw the word and put the book down. So now I had another dear and precious friend that I might offend. This line drawn for me was starting to cost lots of people I loved, but little did I know that all of this was preparing me for what it was going to cost me down the road. God has got us all in training because we are in a war down here. We are fighting for our spiritual life every day and for the lives of our loved ones. It's an unseen battle, so it often seems silly to others when they hear us take a stand when we feel that God is leading us a certain way. Ephesians 6:10-12 states the truth perfectly:

> "Finally, be strong in the Lord and in His mighty power. Put on the full armor of God so that you can take your stand against the devil's schemes. For our struggle is not against flesh and blood, but against the rulers, against the authorities, against the powers of this dark world and against the spiritual forces of evil in the heavenly realms."

Whew! Sounds scary and makes me want to get in bed and cover my head! But I can't—I'm a soldier for my Lord and I want to serve Him with all that is in me. How could I not, since He gave His very life for me?

I told my "bad-word-marking" friend that I still couldn't read the book after all her hard work. I don't think she agreed with me, but she is so kind that she understood that it was important to me, and she respected that.

Wonderful! Now the whole thing was finally over . . . I thought.

I got a text from my sweet Andrew telling me that he had been asked to be in a major production at Western Carolina University playing the guitar. The producer had requested Andrew personally because of his stellar reputation as a guitarist. I was thrilled! I love nothing more than piling in the car with lots of home baked goodies and heading to watch my firstborn perform. Someone once said that they didn't know which they enjoyed more, watching Andrew perform, or watching me watch Andrew perform. I can be a bit demonstrative when it comes to my wonderful children. They are such a joy to me.

As I was talking to Andrew later one night on the phone, he told me that as he had been practicing for the production, he noticed the word "g**d***" was in the play. My heart sank. I **never** thought this line God drew for me would be a line between me and one of my children. I told Andrew that was 'my line' and told him that I felt sick. I changed the subject, got off the phone, and went to my husband and wept. I thought my heart would literally break. I knew I would have to tell Andrew and I dreaded it with everything in me. I needed God's comfort because it hurt so much to hurt one of my children.

I did what I always do, ran to God and His Word. My daily reading was in Isaiah 66. This is what I read in verse two : "This is the one I esteem: he who is humble and contrite in spirit, and trembles at My word." Then in verse five, "Hear the word of the LORD, you who tremble at His word: 'Your brothers who hate you and exclude you because of **My Name** . . ." And finally in verse 13 I read, "As a mother comforts her child, so will I comfort you; and you will be comforted . . ."

God was letting me know that I was to take my stand and depend on Him for my comfort. As much as my children don't understand some of the things I do right now, I know that when I choose to obey God, ultimately, I'm choosing what's best for them too. For me to be in a right relationship with God will put me in a place to be able to let the Spirit of the Living God flow through me, pray through me, and love them in their best interest instead of doing what will make me popular with them. They need God more than they need me and I may be the only person that feels that way. I can't let anything jeopardize that position. I will guard my relationship with God with my whole heart.

Oswald Chambers (1995) puts it best:

"What My Obedience to God Costs Other People"

> *"If we obey God, it is going to cost other people more than it costs us, and that is where the pain begins. If we are in love with our Lord, obedience does not cost us anything—it is a delight. But to those who do not love Him, our obedience does cost a great deal. If we obey God, it will mean that other people's plans are upset. They will ridicule us as if to say, 'You call this Christianity?' We could*

> *prevent the suffering, but not if we are obedient to God. We must let the cost be paid."*

This is the first paragraph of the January 11 reading from the book, "My Utmost for His Highest" and it speaks volumes. I didn't care what it cost me to obey, but I hated to make my child or anybody else feel condemnation. I often quote Matthew 10:37 in my teaching, "If anyone loves son or daughter more than Me then he (or she) is not worthy of Me."

I went down to see Andrew when the time grew close for his performance, and as I was cutting his hair in the dorm bathroom, I told him through tears that I couldn't come watch him because I felt like God had spoken to me about that word. Although he didn't (and doesn't) agree, he was kind and wonderful which made the tears flow even more. Oh, how I love him . . . but I love God more.

Rick and Scott went to the production, and I stayed at home. I decided to stand alone on this one. The show came and went without fanfare. A small blip on the radar of life, but as my pastor says, "Big doors open on small hinges." Who knows what fruit that seemingly small decision will bear someday? That's why it's called faith. You don't get to see what's going to happen immediately; you have to believe that God is at work and trust that He knows best. I know it facilitated some discussion between me and my other sweet boy. He told me that he didn't understand why I couldn't go to something and either walk out during the time that the word was said, or just ignore it since I'm not actually saying it. Good question.

I tried my best to explain. I never get mad when my kids ask me things. I'm nearly fifty years old and didn't realize how important this issue is. Maybe it's because to a degree, I'm desensitized. I told Scott that since I've found out how serious God's Name is to Him, that I really don't want anything to do with a book, a movie, a play, a song, or anything else that takes that **Name** not only in vain, but puts the word d*** after it. If someone uses that word, it shows me how little they value God, and I don't want any part of it. It fills me with indignation.

Scott still didn't see things the way I did and just agreed to disagree. He was nearly 18 when all of this happened and was becoming a man, and he will have to find his way with God and learn how to hear Him himself. As I said, it's taken me half of a lifetime to realize these things. I'm no one to throw stones.

I got up the next morning to talk to God about my talk with Scott. I'll end this story with my daily reading. Call me delusional if you want, but I live in my own world and like it here. Friends know that I often say I love God's Word so much, I would eat it if I could.

<u>Jeremiah 15:16-17</u>

"When Your words came, I ate them; they were my joy and my heart's delight, for I bear Your **Name**, O LORD God Almighty. I never sat in the company of revelers, never made merry with them; I sat alone because Your hand was on me and You had filled me with indignation."

As the song says, "You can have all this world, just give me Jesus."

My Most Painful Story

"But the greatest of these is love . . . ."

I am almost finished writing my book and I have tried several times to write this story. It is the hardest because it encompasses so much.

As I started to follow hard after God, I found I wanted to believe that He loved me so much and had good thoughts toward me, but circumstances kept telling me a different story. I was obeying God, reading the Bible, fasting on occasion, homeschooling my children, teaching Bible studies and truly enjoying doing all of those things. There was only one problem: our family's financial circumstances just seemed to get worse and worse.

My husband changed careers when the kids were all young. He went from being a restaurant manager to being a stock broker. He really needed a working wife to be able to get firmly established financially in that business, but we had decided that I would stay home. My dear husband was trying so hard to have a career that would provide for his family and not be so hard on his body. The restaurant business is definitely best suited for a young person with its long hours and so much time on your feet. I supported him and thought that God would just make us successful since I was such a good and obedient Christian. You see, I thought that was the goal for me—to be good and obedient. But God was after something entirely different: He wanted me to be like His Son. I have a bubbly personality and it seems that people have just naturally liked me all my life. When I became a Christian, I was changed dramatically inside and I saw what a sinful life I had lived. Being so friendly, I found I really didn't need the Holy Spirit's power to seem like a good Christian; acting out that part came easily to me. What I know now is that if God had allowed my circumstances to be easy or my husband to make lots of money, I would have never gone deep with God.

I had three children that were my responsibility—remember that I wasn't just their mother, but I was also their teacher in a homeschool setting—so I couldn't just go to work and deliver myself from the pressure and humiliation of being poor. I wish I could write down what a supportive and loving wife I was early on when life was hard, but I can't. I started to realize how conditional my love was and how shallow I was spiritually. It was very disappointing. I had always thought I was a much better person than I was proving to be, and I suspect that's true of all of us. The fire of suffering forces what you really are to come to the top. Just like the impurity in gold or silver, fire brings the dross to the surface so the refiner can skim it off to make it pure. When he sees his reflection, he knows that the impurities are gone. Well, that is what God does with us. He lets the fires of affliction burn hard and strong because He knows that true happiness is found when my whole being is given over to Him in love and trust, and His Spirit is strong and unhindered in me. Anything else will ultimately bring me misery. I know that now, but I spent many years trying very hard to be better and better so God would take my suffering away. Thank goodness He doesn't conform to my understanding. He remains steady and strong in His perfect love for me and does what's best. Oh, how I love Him!

It has taken me many years to be able to tell Him those simple words and truly mean them. Years ago, I decided that I was going to quit lying to Him, and I started telling Him that I wanted to love Him, but that I knew I really didn't, not the way that I wanted to. He knew it was an issue of trust and trust takes time. I asked Him to take me to the place where I was able to love and trust Him. You know, it's humbling to accept the truth that you can't even love God without His help. The Bible says that 'without Him, I can do nothing'(John 15:5); I believe that now with all my heart. Most people, whether Christian or non-Christian, like to sit around and talk about all the nice things they do and how wonderful and loving they are (especially in comparison to others). I try not to do that anymore, because I know the goodness that is in me is borrowed and I don't want to take credit because it comes from God. It is His glory. If I'm ever cut off from "the Source", darkness will reign in me.

This takes me back to the scripture from I Corinthians 13 that I quoted at the beginning of this story; "the greatest of these is love." When I first wrote this story several years ago, I thought the greatest thing I could give God was faith, so He would bless me and not destroy me. What I know now is that the worst thing He could have done at that time was take my problems away. I would have stayed on the treadmill of faith trying to impress God more and more with what a good girl I was and how faithless I thought my Rick was. You see, I had been told how sweet and wonderful I was most of my life and it took true suffering that went on and on for me to see how ugly I really was inside and having finally seen that, to beg God to get the ugly out of me. I used to think that God didn't want me to **act** mean, but what I found out is that He didn't want me to **be** mean. This may be a shock, but if you don't know how mean you can be without God, you just haven't been in the right circumstances. An eye-opening scripture from the book of Deuteronomy 28:53-57 says it much better than I can:

"Because of the **suffering** that your enemy will inflict on you during the siege, you will eat the fruit of the womb, the flesh of the sons and daughters the LORD your God has given you. Even the most gentle and sensitive man among you will have no compassion on his own brother or the wife he loves or his surviving children, and he will not give to one of them any of the flesh of his children that he is eating. It will be all he has left because of the **suffering** your enemy will inflict on you during the siege of all your cities. The most gentle and sensitive woman among you-so sensitive and gentle that she would not venture to touch the ground with the sole of her foot-will begrudge the husband she loves and her own son or daughter the afterbirth from her womb and the children she bears. For she intends to eat them secretly during the siege and in the distress that your enemy will inflict on you in your cities" (*emphasis mine*).

Strong words, but suffering brings out attitudes and abilities that we never thought we would find within ourselves, some positive and some negative. It can be very humbling. I'm no longer judgmental of others because I have had to see myself guilty before God of terrible thoughts during this particular time in my life. I wanted to blame others, and I would often think about what a great Christian I could be if God would just straighten out everybody around me, especially my husband. Rick wasn't spiritually minded like me, but he had the one thing that mattered more than all my faith put together . . . love. He just loves me and the kids and works himself to death to take care of us, without asking anything in return. He doesn't do nice things so we'll notice and feed his ego; he doesn't even understand that kind of love. He just loves.

Unfortunately, since we didn't have much money, I didn't value his love. I just wanted him to be more successful so I wouldn't have to keep living by faith—and isn't that an ironic thing for a Christian to say? I started to really relate to the Israelites in the desert; they wanted to hurry and get to the Promised Land so they could take care of themselves and not depend on God for everything. He didn't do things to suit them and they wanted to regain control of their lives, but God happened to be their only source of food and water. They hated that because, after The Fall, mankind's greatest desire has been to be free from dependence on anyone (especially God), to always be in control, and be able make their own decisions about their future.

You may be familiar with Beth Moore's Bible study called "Breaking Free." I think the first time I facilitated that study was around 1999. One of the questions required naming a weakness that you have. I wrote down that I can give to people, but I absolutely won't take. I remember thinking to myself that God was probably proud that my biggest fault was such a good one. I mean, who wants to be a taker? When my kids were small, I prided myself on never asking for help. They were **my** kids and I wasn't going to ask others to keep them or help me with them. I would always keep anyone else's children if they needed it, but I always let people know that I didn't need for them to do anything for me. I didn't want to be a bother. I was self-sufficient. But what I didn't realize then was that pride was the root of the way I felt. I mean that with all my heart. Never needing anyone for anything is an issue deeply rooted in pride and a need to control. Of course God condemns laziness and mooching; He even says that if a man doesn't work, he shouldn't eat. But to never accept help emotionally, physically or monetarily because you are too proud to do so is wrong. God even allowed Jesus to be supported during His ministry by some prominent women. To think that God sent His Son into the world and made Him dependent on others shows how much God wants us to live in close relationships and be dependent on one another.

As I started to truly grow in my faith, I thought the fact that I could talk big about God meant that I was a spiritual giant. I was at the kitchen counter one day doing dishes and I felt like God gave me a wonderful truth concerning Rick. I felt like He said to me, "I have more respect for Rick because he is cold, while you are lukewarm. At least he doesn't fake it like you." I immediately knew what Scripture passage God meant; it was verses 15 and 16 from the third chapter of the book of Revelations: "I know your deeds, that you are neither cold nor hot. I wish you were either one or the other. So, because you are lukewarm—neither hot nor cold—I am about to spit you out of My mouth." I had never considered that scripture from Revelation in that light. It never dawned on me that God would **prefer** cold to lukewarm; I only thought He wanted people that were 'hot'. When God revealed that to me, I wanted to jump for joy because there is always joy (even in conviction) when it is really God speaking to you. He doesn't tell you things to just hurt you; He is telling you something that will set you free . . . from yourself. That is true freedom. How sad that God tries to tell His children the truth, but they make excuses and blame others. They are putting another brick in the walls of their own little prisons.

I know I sound ruthless when talking about myself and my heart issues, but that is because I've found that God is. He sees blackness all through us and longs to set us free and yet we fight Him tooth and nail, all the while thinking that our husbands, wives, kids, friends, jobs, etc. are the problem, when the real problem is inside us. He uses all the external circumstances to reveal to us who we really are. They are the heat source that God uses to bring the truth about us to the surface, as the refiner uses the heat of the fire. No one else can put venom into us—that comes from our own inner man.

And here's another truth—what's in your heart eventually comes out of your mouth. We may not say what we really think directly to the person who is the subject of our mental outburst, but we will say how we feel to others through gossip. We murder people with our tongues. The book of James says, "The tongue is also a fire, a world of evil among the parts of the body. It corrupts the whole person, sets the whole course of his life on fire, and is itself set on fire by hell." It goes on to say, "With the tongue we praise our Lord and Father, and with it we curse men, who have been made in God's likeness. Out of the same mouth come praise and cursing. My brothers, this should not be."

Now I realize when I say mean things about anybody, I have a problem between me and God. If Jesus lived and loved by the power of the Holy Spirit and I have that same Spirit in me, then I should be empowered to love all people, even my enemies. Jesus did, Stephen did, Paul did, and I could go on listing men and women who loved people in truth and it cost them their lives. They loved others more than themselves. They didn't tell people what they wanted to hear so they would like them and speak well of them. They told them what would make them look at themselves and cry out to God for salvation. That's true love.

Growing up in a family where the women usually controlled the home, and by and large were a little on the man-hating side, when I let the Holy Spirit truly start to dig deep in me, I think I heard something akin to "Houston, we have a problem." I used to visit with my family and when I would see the interactions between husbands and wives, I would think to myself, *"Lord, I may not say it out loud, but I feel all those spiteful and horrible things that the women in my family say."* God doesn't hold the circumstances we were raised in against us, but once we have His Spirit living in us, there is no excuse if we continue that same path. People get upset because the Bible says that God punishes the children to the third and fourth generation of those that hate Him (a little explanation here: I have heard Beth Moore say that "punish" is not as accurate as 'dumped in our laps' . . . meaning we can't help what was handed to us), but He blesses those who love Him to the thousandth generation. I now love Him, so that means that my descendants will be blessed until Jesus returns. A thousand generations will take a long time. The minute I said a big 'yes' to God's salvation and His plans for me, my children were switched to the 'blessed' place in this world. That thrills me and makes me want to bow down and worship this King called Jesus. The blessing of knowing Him intimately is overwhelming.

Through God's Spirit in me, I started to cry out for real and unconditional love for the wonderful man that God not only gave me, but gave me twice (you can find that story a few pages back in this book). I discovered an enemy within me that kept me at arm's length from Rick and fought against giving myself completely to him. That enemy was strong, and convinced me to keep my mask that made me feel safe and secure instead of weak and vulnerable.

Looking back at old prayer journals, I see over and over again that I cried out to God to make me 'one' with Him 'down any road and at any cost'. Although I was afraid, I started to realize that I didn't have forever to get to truly know and trust God. I now realize that was (and still is) His Spirit in me that longed for that union. Jesus prayed that very thing for us before He went to the cross and Jesus gets what He asks. A true child of God will not be satisfied with less. There will be a holy restlessness inside if you have His Spirit. The key to intimacy with Rick and love for him was intimacy with God and love for Him. We will never love another human the right way unless God's love is the source. When it's tainted with our self-life, it is tainted indeed. We will pour out our love on certain people, but then we will stand with our little cup and ask them to fill it back up. How foolish when instead, we can have God's Living Water filling us to overflowing and never even worry if we get something in return! It's supernatural and intoxicating to be full of God's love. As I heard Bill Stafford say, "I never quit drinking, I just changed fountains." God offers the most wretched of sinners and anyone else, for that matter, who will come to Him, an endless supply of Living Water. Listen to how seriously God takes our refusal: "Be appalled at this, O heavens, and shudder with great horror," declares the LORD. "My people have committed two sins: They have forsaken Me, the spring of living water, and have dug their own cisterns, broken cisterns that cannot hold water" (Jeremiah 2:12-13). We are so proud that we think we can live a self-centered life and have good marriages on our own. If your source of love for your husband or wife is void of the Living Water (the Holy Spirit), you will either start to despise that person for not fulfilling you or cling to them as your only hope for security and happiness and you'll suffocate the life out of them. Actually, you will probably do both of these things to some degree. When we cling to people as our idols, we will ultimately hate them. This is one of the reasons that the first commandment forbids having other gods. Those commands were given because they reflect our God's wonderful nature and show us that He longs for us to have joy overflowing. Only He knows what will give us true joy because true joy is only found in being like Him.

There is a verse in the book of Proverbs that states "The wicked borrow and do not repay." Before I go any further in this story, I want to say that I am not excusing or trying to over-spiritualize what happened to us financially. I am just writing down what happened, as it unfolded, so that you can see how God works in the middle of big messes. God does not cause us to sin, but He uses every circumstance in our lives to reach us and draw us into intimacy with Himself. God wrote down the truth about His people in the Bible for a good reason—we are sinners who lose our way, go down wrong paths, make huge mistakes, but He takes pity on us and uses it **all** to bring us close to Him. He doesn't want statues in a museum; He wants real people who know they need Him and can't make it without Him.

As you could see from my "Christmas Story", times were very lean in 2002 and things were not getting better; they were getting worse, much worse. I was doing a few things trying to make extra money, but between homeschooling my kids, trying to help my precious mother-in-law as she cared for my father-in-law during his battle with cancer, teaching exercise, discipling many women, and trying to keep my head above my own laundry, at times I thought that I wasn't going to make it. If I hadn't experienced God the way I did when I surrendered all to Him in 1996, I would have lost heart, but I didn't. I knew the power of The Holy Spirit in a profound way. The release of God's Spirit and power in me made me very hungry to read His Word, and as I read and studied my Bible, I saw that what God was allowing to happen to me was the same thing that He had allowed to happen to His servants in the past. Moses was a great and powerful man in Egypt, but then spent 40 years in the desert tending sheep as a nobody before God allowed him to be "His man" to lead His people out of Egypt. Joseph was the spoiled and chosen son of his father but God let him be sold as a slave, falsely accused of a sexual crime, and put in prison for several years to prepare his character to be the second in command of the greatest nation on the earth at that time, Egypt. I saw that even though Joseph had these things done to him, he wasn't a victim. He was in the center of God's permissive will and what everyone around him meant for evil, God meant it for good. That showed me (in theory) that I wasn't a victim, but that in the middle of what looked so haphazard and crazy in my life, God was weaving a beautiful tapestry. I was trying with all my heart to have the faith to believe that because what I was seeing was telling me that the Bible was a lie and that I was crazy for believing in this God. Circumstances were yelling in my ear, "You better get a job and save up some money or you are going down. Your kids and everyone else are going to see that there is nothing to this 'God thing' that you talk about all the time."

I often write notes in the margins of my Bible, and one such note is written beside the words in Micah 4:10. The Scripture verse reads: "Writhe in agony, O daughter of Zion, like a woman in labor, for now you must leave the city to camp in the open field. You will go to Babylon; there you will be rescued. There the LORD will redeem you out of the hand of your enemies." Beside it, I wrote: "4-19-03, asking about debt situation." I had learned to hear God's voice to some degree and definitely was feeling that He was giving me His plan. But how could I marry that with "For I know the plans I have for you," declares the Lord, "plans to prosper you and not to harm you, plans to give you hope and a future" (Jeremiah 29:11)? We Americans think that prosperity almost always means money, but I think money has very little to do with prosperity. What makes me rich is God's presence, period. I had His presence, but I wanted more of it, and I wanted my husband and my children to believe God was real, not in theory but in reality. I told Him that I wanted His will and plans for us no matter what and I meant it—even if it meant losing everything.

I looked in scripture to see if God told people bad news like this before it happened and I found this warning in Acts 20:22-24: "And now, compelled by the Spirit, I am going to Jerusalem, not knowing what will happen to me there. I only know that in every city the Holy

Spirit **warns** me that **prison** and **hardships** are facing me. However, I consider my life worth nothing to me, if only I may finish the race and complete the task the Lord Jesus has given me—the task of testifying to the gospel of God's grace" *(emphasis mine).* God's people are compelled to do His will because we have another Person inside of us that longs to please the Father, and that Person is the Holy Spirit. That is nothing less than a miracle because it goes against our nature to suffer on any level, much less when we won't get glory in the eyes of the world. Our nature would probably go through suffering for a loved one or for our children and might even reluctantly go through suffering for friends if it knows that it will get stroked and admired, but human nature will never willingly suffer for people *who* hate us, especially if there will be no earthly recognition to boot. Getting everything we want 'in Jesus Name' will never convince a lost world that God is real. Suffering horribly yet continuing to praise God and love people—now that is nothing short of a real miracle. Why else would the thief on the cross become convinced that Jesus was "the One" who held the key to his salvation? At first, the thief's suffering caused him to spew venom out on Jesus, but watching a man suffer just like he was and seeing firsthand true love and compassion pouring out of that Man changed his mind and turned a hardened criminal into a humble and broken man asking Jesus to remember him when He came into His kingdom. Can you imagine looking over to our precious Jesus asking for salvation after cursing Him and seeing those eyes look back with all that love in them and hearing the words, "I tell you the truth, today you will be with me in paradise" (Luke 23:43).

I love what Paul says in Philippians 3:10, "I want to know Christ and the power of His resurrection and the fellowship of sharing in His sufferings, becoming **like** Him in His death . . ." (*emphasis mine*). God wants me to be so purified through suffering and glory that I truly become **like** Him. That will mean people can hate me and hurl insults and even kill me, and nothing but truth and love will pour out. Think that sounds impossible? Read the account of Stephen in the seventh chapter of Acts. Because he was full of the Holy Spirit, when he was being stoned by people who hated him, he cried out, "Lord, don't hold this sin against them!" Oh, how that gives me hope that God can truly make me (a wretch) pure in heart!

So, obviously, purity of heart is the goal of God for His children, and a pure heart will be full of God, and if my heart is full of God, it will be full of love since God is love. Sadly though, my suffering brought so much bitterness, anger, unbelief, and jealousy over the good fortune of others to the surface in me. Of course, I tried not to show it, but I definitely started to see what I was really made of in ways that would have stayed neatly hidden without this heat from the refiner's fire. He didn't listen to my heart's cry for relief, although I know He heard it. I started to feel like I didn't care if I got any holier, if I could just go buy the kids underwear and have a guarantee of enough money to buy groceries each week. Today, I'm thankful that God answered my prayer of "down any road and at any cost" and didn't listen when I wanted Him to stop, and how I praise Him that He didn't leave all that junk inside me!

The truth was that I was spiritually very immature and didn't realize it. I thought I had great faith until the bank account was dry and credit cards started to be maxed out. I found out that there were a couple of little people in me called "Ms. Atheist" and "Ms. Self-Pity" and they were trying to constantly whisper in my ear things like, "You have been such a good Christian. If God is real why would He let this suffering come to you like this? You wouldn't do this to your children." Better yet, "God must just be mean. You are so tired and you take care of so many people, teach Bible studies, are a great wife, never complain, blah, blah, blah." I tried to block those voices out, but they threatened to overtake me. Thankfully, I was reading my Bible and staying in the Word, and I kept crying out to Him to get me to the place of intimacy with Him and love for Him, and to fill me with Holy Spirit love for my husband. I was sick of conditional, performance-based love—the kind of love I'd known and felt all my life.

I would try to talk Rick into being more spiritual and I would get mad when he didn't go to church. I felt like God started going to the heart of my requests and asking me why I wanted Rick to be more spiritual and why I wanted him at church. You can't lie to the Holy Spirit because He doesn't ask questions in order to get an answer; He asks in order to lead you into Truth. He has His ways of getting you to the conclusion that He wants you to reach and opening your eyes. I saw that my motive for Rick was not love, but my own comfort. I thought that if he would become a man of deep faith, he would not only be closer to God but more importantly, he would finally appreciate what a wonderful and faith-filled woman he had been fortunate enough to have all those years—maybe even facilitating a "Terri Day" at church one Sunday. I could see and hear it all in my mind—Rick would give a speech singing my praises for being a "Proverbs 31 Woman" while he was sitting watching football on Sunday, and then go on to say how he saw God in me daily and how unworthy he was. Secondly, if he would fall down and worship God (and me, while he was at it), then our money problems would be over and I could give testimony about how we tithed and God blessed us so much that we support various and sundry charities, naming each one I'm sure. Thirdly, since I taught women's Bible study classes about submission to your husband, I could also talk about how God will make all your problems disappear if you obey God and your husband perfectly. But for some reason, God just wasn't giving me everything I was asking for. (Can anybody relate?)

As I said earlier, I did have faith (or was trying hard to), but true Holy Spirit love was proving elusive in the midst of so much hardship. You won't convince God to change His ways or take short cuts for you, but the following passage, II Peter 1:5-7, clearly shows the journey from faith to love: "For this very reason, make every effort to add to your **faith**, goodness; and to goodness, knowledge; and to knowledge, self-control; and to self-control, perseverance; and to perseverance, godliness; and to godliness; brotherly kindness; and to brotherly kindness, **love** (*emphasis mine*)." Whew! Finally got to love. Look at the journey! It's long and full of things like 'making every effort', 'knowledge', and 'perseverance.' It's not a walk in the park. It's the fight of your life to get to the goal of love, which according to I Corinthians 13 is all that matters in the end.

Since God started to teach me how important His love pouring through me was and is, I asked four friends (each with difficult husband-wife relationships) to fast and pray once a week with me for each other and our husbands. I asked them to ask God to change me and Rick instead of our circumstances and no matter how hot it all got that He would enable me to stay firm and unmoved in the midst of it. I really felt like God wanted to give me love and wanted to give Rick faith. I had one and he had the other. I sensed God saying to me that I was to start treating Rick as if he were the best provider, husband and father in the world. Coming from my background, that was a big request. I told God that I couldn't do that for Rick—not at that point in my life—but I would do it for Him. I started to serve Rick and treat him as nicely as I would treat a guest at my home. We can all be nice to visitors, or even people in a drive-through window by choice, even if we are having a bad day. Could I not be nice and kind to the person who was the father of my children and who the Bible says I'm one flesh with? I also felt like God posed this question to me, "Since you claim to Rick that you are full of The Holy Spirit (aka God), based on how you treat him and love him, how much would he surmise that I love him?" I was ashamed. Granted, most of my sin may have been hidden in self-righteous judgment in my heart, but that doesn't make it less of a sin. God only cares about what is in my heart because that's who I really am. I have sons of my own and I wondered how I would feel if the women they married didn't love, respect and value them. I was beginning to understand why Jesus said we have to "hate our own life" to follow Him. In comparison to His holiness and love, mine was base and hateful. I wanted free, as Paul said in Romans 7, from this body of death. I started to look at my man with different eyes. I saw that God created every part of him and he was a work of art to God. I started to use my words to build him up and encourage him instead of letting him know how disappointed I was in him and our circumstances.

I saw that if I believed that God was all He said He is in the Bible, why would I look to Rick to meet all of our needs? The Bible says some pretty impressive things about God's power like, "He made the stars also", as if that's a footnote in the creation story. I asked myself the question, "If God spoke and created everything, why am I so worried?" I had to answer honestly and say that unbelief was my real enemy, not money or Rick's inability to support us on what he was making. God said of the Israelites when they were in the desert that they would never enter His rest because of unbelief. I came to understand that "unbelief" for the Israelites didn't mean they didn't believe in God. Obviously they did believe in God; after all, they saw many miracles on their journey and even had manna rained down daily for food. Their unbelief concerned the goodness of God. They didn't believe He was good and had good intentions toward them. I realized that was my real enemy also. I stopped judging the Israelites so harshly as I read my Bible. I saw that I was just as grouchy and hateful as they were. When things went great, they were on a spiritual high, but when they were hungry or thirsty, they were sure that God had brought them to the desert to kill them. Their view of God changed every time their circumstances did. When things were good—"He loves me"—but when they weren't—"He loves me not." Their sin of blaspheming God's character cost them the promised land and their future. I didn't want to pay such a price for me, Rick or my kids.

As my eyes were opened to glorious truth, and I started to cry out for deliverance from my rotten self, some truly awesome things started to happen—and the stories in this book are the record of those things. As God poured out suffering on me, He was being faithful to start answering amazing prayers and let me see His glory through my tear-stained and grateful eyes. I wasn't the same little cocky wife asking Rick why he wouldn't go to church. In seeing my own faithlessness deep in my heart coupled with my pride about how full of faith I thought I was, I was just glad God hadn't struck me dead.

Remember a few pages back where I quoted the passage from Micah 4:10, the passage that I believed God had given me with regard to our financial situation? That scripture had said that I would "writhe in agony." Check. I was doing lots of writhing and agonizing. I can't think of any two words that fit what was happening any better than those two. God is very precise in everything He does. We couldn't pay our bills. Car payments were late, foreclosure was being threatened, and credit card payments were the lowest priority so they were very hit and miss. We were barely keeping our heads above water in the financial realm, but Rick was watching God provide food for our table through my prayers. God was showing Rick His power and giving him faith all while giving me Holy Spirit, unconditional love. Oh the joy of being a conduit of the love of God! I see now why God says that if my faith can move mountains and I don't have love, I am nothing. I think my writhing and agonizing was kind of akin to a snake trying to shed its skin. It agonizes and writhes but it is getting free from that restrictive and ill-fitting thing, so it can be free. I was shedding this "body of death."

The second part of my scripture was: ". . . for now you must leave the city to camp in the open field."

I thought that meant foreclosure on our house. We were a pretty pessimist group growing up in my family and that tendency was still there no matter how hard I fought it. I just felt sure that what the scripture meant about an open field was that we would suffer the open shame of publicly losing our home. Since credit card payments were lowest on the priority list, one wasn't being paid at all. I didn't know what to do, so I did nothing. I told almost no one about all that was happening, but I did confide part of it to a dear friend that I respect and trust. This faithful friend gave me advice that seemed to come straight out of the third chapter of the book of Ecclesiastes: "To everything there is a season, a time for every purpose under heaven." She reminded me that there was a time to wait and a time to act, and she suggested that this may be the time when I needed to get a job and start delivering myself. Knowing that she loved me and wanted only the best for my family, I listened to her words, and they made sense humanly speaking, so I prayerfully and carefully considered them. As part of that consideration, I dug into God's Word, which reminded me that Rick is the priest of our home and the head. I am his helper. My main role is keeper of the home, wife and mother. I am the gatekeeper of my children's lives and souls and I didn't take leaving that post lightly.

I believe that the Bible is relevant to every situation known to man. When anyone reads a story in the Bible, I believe it speaks to that specific reader's situation. I know that my friend shares that belief. But since we can never know all the facts about another person's situation, what may seem to be good advice to us may not actually be the right advice for someone else. So while what my friend advised did make sense in a very practical way, I came to understand that it wasn't the action I was meant to take at that time. I know that I've given advice over the years that was, like my friend's, grounded in Scripture, but in the end, the final decision and personal interpretation of that Scripture is between the individual believer and God, something that we have to understand and accept.

Those words in Micah are pretty strong words and I had to cling to the Word of God very tightly to not give into the temptation to just give up on Rick being able to lead our family. I had taught many women to believe that God could work in spite of their husbands and now I had to practice what I preached in a real way. I found it was easy talking it but hard living it, but what good is what I teach if it is untested and I don't really believe it to my core? God let the fire blaze on. I'm reading the book *Safely Home*, by Randy Alcorn (2011) now and he says that "real gold fears no fire." I longed to be real gold, pure gold. The fire had to get hotter. Sometimes we go through things that are not just for us in the present moment, but for our destiny. How could Joseph have known during those lonely times, sitting in a horrible prison, that God was preparing him for greatness? God's idea of greatness will always involve humility. The great people in the Bible accepted God's road to humility while the people that ended up as colossal failures were the ones who tried to be great while keeping their pride intact. That attempt has never been successful and never will be. I also saw that their roads to humility involved things that were beyond their control. It wasn't my fault that I wasn't the head of our home. I'm not saying I could have done a better job and that's not even my point. My point is that I didn't grab the wheel from Rick and try to drive. I just sat in the passenger's seat and prayed and tried with all my heart to trust God's heart.

God taught me an important thing about covenants during this time also. God made a covenant with mankind and promised to redeem us. He didn't do anything wrong at any time, but because of our sin, He had to die a horrible death. I started to think about how He treated all of us as He suffered and died, and I saw that He loved us and treated us with compassion, kindness and forgiveness. He wanted me to treat Rick the same way even though I was suffering horribly because of our financial mess.

It all started to come to a head in June of 2003. I was at my neighbor's house caring for her elderly father while she was at work when I saw the police pull up in my driveway. Praise God we were all over there because my sweet children were protected from knowing what was going on. It was a summons to go to court for an unpaid credit card. By this point, I was just in the acceptance mode. This problem was so big that there was nobody to fix it and nowhere to hide. It was either God or I was going down. What a position of power! If I could have fixed it, I would have but I would have missed finding out who this God is that I now know and have the privilege of being in a relationship with!

Our court day was scheduled weeks before Tataw died, and it happened to fall on the Wednesday after we buried him on Tuesday. As you read in "Tataw's Story", God parted the Red Sea, figuratively speaking for all of us, so He was being faithful to kill me on one hand and thrill me on the other. His perfection is mind boggling.

Because of what I had experienced through Tataw's salvation and Andrew playing his guitar for him, I knew I was in the exact center of God's permissive will and He had a plan for me. I felt special and loved even though I was going through one of the most difficult things I could imagine. I was so sweet to Rick on our way there and was trying to make him not feel bad while we were waiting for the court session to begin. Since I had never had anything like this happen to me before, I didn't think I would know anyone there, and was hoping we could get in and out unnoticed. When the magistrate walked in, I thought to myself how glad I was to get this started so this nightmare could end. The magistrate walked up to her chair and when she turned around, I saw that it was a friend of mine! She wasn't someone that I went to lunch with or anything like that, but I was her hairdresser and we had talked in depth about our relationships with Christ since she was a Christian too. I was mortified and turned to Rick and said, "I know her! She is a friend that used to have great respect for me and my walk with God."

Trying to keep things light-hearted, my Rick said, "Oh well, this will be part of our testimony someday." I felt like God was speaking the truth through Rick without him even knowing it.

My scripture had said that I would be "in an **open field**." I couldn't have described it any better. Nowhere to hide, I was out in plain sight. That five minutes or so in front of my friend did more to burn away my pride than all the previous seven years or so of daily Bible study and prayer. Praise God for His precision laser that cuts out that horrific cancer that is His enemy inside me. I mentor women, teach Bible study, lead retreats for women, and speak at area churches, and I witness firsthand what pride is doing in our churches and our relationships. Our 'rights' are killing the life of God in us. The book of Philippians 2:5-8, tells us that our "attitude should be the same as that of Christ Jesus. Who being in very nature God, did not consider equality with God something to be grasped, but made Himself **nothing**, taking the very nature of a **servant** being made in human likeness. And being found in appearance as a man, He humbled Himself and became obedient to death, even death on a cross!" *(emphasis mine)*. God in human flesh made Himself nothing! Just who do we think we are?

Rick told me that I could go outside and he would go up by himself. I said that if Jesus Christ wasn't ashamed to stand with me then I wasn't ashamed to stand with him. Our names were called and we walked up together. My sweet Rick started talking (very unusual because he is a man of few words), and he took the entire blame for why we were there. The magistrate looked on the documents and since my signature was there too, I was guilty also. I tried to say something spiritual and just sounded kind of dumb I'm sure.

I was fellowshipping in the sufferings of Christ in a strange way. Of course, Jesus never sinned by not paying bills so I don't mean that. We were guilty, and of course Jesus was never guilty of anything. But God's covenant with mankind made Him guilty by association (He **became** sin). People looked at His suffering and considered Him "stricken by God and afflicted" and He didn't defend Himself. I'm sure I looked like a fraud and a loser to my friend and maybe even like God was punishing me. That's what people thought about Jesus as He hung there on the cross.

I quoted part of this passage from Philippians earlier, but now I was seeing the truth of the entire thing. He didn't want me just to be like Him inside, but to count everything else, even my reputation as rubbish. If people knew the joy that comes from completely giving all control of their lives to God, they would run to Him as fast as they could. But you won't get the joy until you go through the pain. Sadly, most people will see the cost and not be willing to pay it. "But whatever was to my profit I now consider loss for the sake of Christ. What is more, I consider

everything loss compared to the surpassing greatness of knowing Christ Jesus my Lord, for whose sake I have lost all things. I consider them rubbish, that I may gain Christ and be found in Him not having a righteousness of my own that comes from the law, but that which is through faith in Christ—the righteousness that comes from God and is by faith. I want to **know** Christ and the **power** of His resurrection and the fellowship of **sharing** in His **sufferings**, becoming like Him in His death . . . ." (Philippians 3:7-10, *emphasis mine*). Power on one hand and suffering on the other, all the while being made truly like Him—that is the privilege of being a child of God. Your greatest need, and mine as well, is to shed this sinful nature and share in the divine nature. Oh the glory of what God offers us if we will do it His way!

We left the courthouse. The facts were now public, the truth was now known. The representative from the bank that owned the credit card was in the courtroom. He and Rick talked and they were able to work out a payment agreement. Since the agreement was made voluntarily on both sides, no ruling needed to be issued by the magistrate. Soon after all of this took place, I prayed about a job and I went to work for Shelly (another story in this book). I also prayed about sending the kids to school and a scholarship was provided. Those two things (leaving the kids and putting them in school) were my greatest fears and God had not touched those before. I found that He leaves no stone unturned and will leave no place of fear and unbelief untouched. Wanting to guard the hearts and lives of my children and keep them home would seem to be a fine and noble thing, but I realized that if I was doing that mainly out of fear, God wasn't going to bless that. He wants all I do to be done because I love and trust Him, not because I'm afraid of "the world" tainting my kids. Their enemy, just like mine, is inside of them, not outside. You can't sequester your kids into holiness and every homeschool mom knows what I'm talking about when I say that. I think we all want the safety of the "God formula", so our kids will turn out right. God didn't want me to think that the only way He could work in my family was the "homeschool, stay-at-home mom" way. He wanted me to follow Him and obey Him, not a formula. We teach our formulas instead of reliance and oneness with Him when our formulas work, but what about when those formulas don't work? What do we teach then? I didn't leave my post out of fear, but let God call me away in faith believing that He knew best and would take care of my babies.

It was hard for me to believe that God didn't intend for me to keep control of anything in my life, or the lives of my children, but that was and is precisely what He intended and intends. What a mistake we make when we think we have to shield our children from all pain for them to know and trust God. Becca was eight when this happened and it was so painful for her at that time, that had I not had such a direct answer to the prayer about school, I never would have made it. She was so attached to me that it traumatized her to leave home and be in a school situation. When her little eyes would open each morning, tears would start to flow and her stomach would hurt. The amazing thing was that she knew that God had provided a scholarship for school, so she never asked not to go. She trusted that I would keep hearing from God and that He would do what was best. What a horrible thing it is to teach your kids that God won't allow suffering. We parents would remove all pain and cripple our children if left to our own devices. What we have to understand is that God has their best interest at heart too. Now my eyes are open to see that everything in our lives is ordained by God to bring us to the place where we trust His perfect love, even though we don't understand what is going on.

Andrew was in high school and still being schooled at home, so I had another great need since I wasn't home as much. I needed someone to teach Andrew how to do a research paper and a homeschool English class opened up that year. It was as if God was emptying my arms of all the things that I held tightly and fearfully, and putting me in His arms and providing at every turn. I can now say without hesitation that I trust God with my children. Let Him pry your fingers off of them and give them to Him; they are only truly safe in His arms, not yours.

Rick was amazed and astounded and even asked me one day if I was writing all these things down. Our finances were still a mess, so this was the point that I asked Rick if he would sell his beloved BMW to Shelly so we could catch up our house payment. A friend who had no idea I had offered Shelly our car the day before, stopped by and told me that she felt God leading her to pay off Rick's car for us. Not only was Rick's faith growing, so was mine. Thank God I stood firm and didn't let fear rule me when I was tempted to take control of our lives and finances, so the suffering would end prematurely. Little did I know that deliverance truly was right around the corner.

Now, back to that passage from the book of Micah! The last part of my scripture was: "You will go to Babylon; there you will be rescued. There the LORD will redeem you out of the hand of your enemies."

Babylon represented captivity to Israel and we were definitely captive to debt. Proverbs even warns that the borrower is servant to the lender. How true God's Word is! God told Israel that they would go into captivity but He would redeem them from the hand of their enemies. As you can see from this story, God was delivering me from many enemies. The worst enemies that a New Testament believer has are not external enemies, but internal ones. I thought debt was my enemy, but not having a pure heart was the true enemy. The greatest miracle that God can do besides save a soul from hell is to save us from ourselves. To enable us to be like Christ and become nothing, and to truly be a servant expecting nothing in return, getting all our needs (and more) completely satisfied by God Himself is unexplainable and something that only God can do. And that, my friend, is what we were made for. Just sitting here, trying to put down in words what it means to have the gift of being full to overflowing with the Spirit of the Living God is something that I find nearly impossible. It was and is worth anything and everything that He has and will allow in my life. I still don't have money and my car is nearly twenty years old and I'm the happiest person I know, and I'm the richest person I know. I don't say that because I have wonderful children and a great husband (although both of those things happen to be true); I say that because I can say with the prophet Jeremiah, "Let not the wise man boast in his wisdom or the strong man boast of his strength or the rich man boast in his riches, but let him who boasts boast about this; that he understands and knows me, that I am the LORD who exercises kindness, justice and righteousness on earth, for in these I delight, declares the LORD" (Jeremiah 9:23-24). Wow! Just the fact that God Almighty would allow a worm like me to know and understand Him on any level (not completely—no human ever will) is beyond my comprehension. If Christians really understood what the Bible offers, we wouldn't go around with frowns on our faces like life is just so hard and we are so misunderstood. What a slap in the face of God! We should have a robust and active faith. If you don't, go on a journey to find God and don't stop until you hear from Him and never, ever stop hearing from Him.

I had gotten my 'word' from God in April of 2003 and it was now May of 2004. God had done so much but it still looked like we would lose our home. I was waiting on God to redeem me (and by the way, did you know that the word redeem actually means to "buy you out"?). I couldn't figure out how in the world He was going to do that. I still wasn't telling anybody about what was going on with us. I had only told that one friend some bits and pieces but she didn't know the whole story. I hadn't told my family or Rick's family. As a matter of fact, if any of them read this book, this story will probably blow their minds because many of them still don't know. I looked at it like this: if I went around telling everybody about our situation and they all pooled their resources together, had fundraisers and yard sales and barely pulled us out of our pit, where would the glory of God be in that? If God was my Father and owned the whole world, was He not completely cognizant of every hair on my head **and** every dollar owed? To go around all sulky and pitiful would be akin to me making God look like a negligent Father. I'm also not saying that God can't use fundraisers to help people. In my case, He had told me that **He** would redeem me, and I didn't feel like He wanted me to go that route.

To make my point, what if I had a houseful of everything my children could ever need, but I had to watch them go from neighbor to neighbor begging for food and clothing because I was so stingy and mean that I didn't take care for them? God wants real trust from all of us and I was determined to believe in God's goodness even if I didn't understand how or when relief was going to come. At one point during this time, I just looked up to God in my confusion (because at times it felt to me as if I were an orphan who didn't belong to Him at all), and I said to Him, "I will serve You for the rest of my life if the only time I see Your face is before You send me to hell." That may sound crazy because I am a true Christian, but prolonged suffering can make you doubt yourself, your salvation and your sanity. I was just making sure that God knew that I wasn't going away. He was stuck with me and I was never leaving Him, even if He never did anything else for me while I was on this planet. I know that's backward theology because God is holding onto us, but I'm writing what was going on in my heart, and I'm telling the truth, not just saying 'the right thing'.

I owed some doctor bills at this time and I sent what little bit of money I had to pay them off. It was a little over a hundred dollars, and I was just hoping that God would see my act of faith and help us cover what I sent. As the day wore on and I didn't get a check in the mail and no one showed up at my door, I started to really doubt myself. I was thinking that I had gone too far in trying to live by faith and now I wouldn't be able to buy groceries. I felt presumptuous and silly. Maybe all those Christian biographies had gone to my head. Could I really live like my heroes—Corrie ten Boom, George Mueller, Hudson Taylor, just to name a few? Maybe they were special, and normal people like me couldn't depend on God like they could. Let me say right now—that is a lie from the pit! God has no favorites. He will take anybody as far as they are willing to go with Him. The only prerequisite is that you have to die to all desires but for Him.

As I was up late thinking that I had made a huge financial mistake, the phone rang. It was 11:00 pm; no one ever called me that late unless it was an emergency. I ran to get the phone and it was a close friend of mine. She inquired about a mutual friend of ours and was kind of making small talk. She then asked me what was wrong, saying that God wouldn't let her go to bed until she called me. I started to cry and poured out all that was happening in our lives. She told me to write down all of our monthly bills and to be at her house around lunch time the next day, when she would be home after work. Rick was working late, so I sat on our bed and starting writing down all the information I knew. The only problem was that I had no idea what all of our bills were. Rick took care of all our finances, so I was clueless about so many things. I wrote down what I could find and what little I knew and then went to bed very hopeful that our redemption was drawing near.

I got up the next morning and started schooling the kids as usual, all the while wondering how I was going to fill in all those missing blanks in our budget. Rick had gotten home late that night and left early that morning, plus I didn't want to tell him what was going on until I had more details. My friend might just tell us that our situation was way over her head too. I didn't want to give Rick false hope because God had brought me to the place where I wanted to protect him, not crush him. One of my kids needed a particular book that day, so I headed to the garage to see if I could find it. I climbed over some stuff to get to a dusty plastic bin in the corner and as I got close, I noticed a piece of notebook paper just lying on top of the bin I was getting ready to open. When I picked it up, I saw that it was our family budget written in Rick's handwriting with every piece of information that I needed to be able to talk to my friend. To this day, neither Rick nor I know how or why that paper was sitting way back there on a bin that I would never have been anywhere near if, by the sovereignty of God, I hadn't needed a book! I thought to myself when I picked it up, "This is going to be big."

My friend came home from work and I went over to her house. If humility was something you could actually touch and feel, I truly had it, because it felt as real as a sweater draped over my shoulders or a scarf covering my head. If you ever get the humility that God wants for you on any level, it is amazingly real, almost tangible. I wish I could say that I completely embraced the feeling but I was ashamed to have to open this ugly and festering wound of debt and let my healthy friend look in. But she was so precious, kind and gentle as she unwrapped it all and started to wash it out and look at it closely. It had been figuratively taped and bandaged a long time. She carefully cleaned it, put medicine on it, and wrapped it back up the right way. She figured out a way to pay off my car little by little to repair damage done to our credit, and then she paid off the rest of our credit cards and gave me money to replace the money I'd just sent to the doctor. I just sat there feeling humiliated as she cancelled debt after debt for me. I now knew why the Bible says that it is more blessed to give than to receive. I would have given anything to be able to switch places with her, to do what she was doing instead of having to receive. What little bit of pride I still had—and some was still there, believe it or not—was just getting stomped to the ground. I just cried and cried. She got up and hugged me so tightly and said something I will never forget: "Giving money is easy; you've given your life. If you couldn't pay your bills you would still go to heaven. If you hadn't laid down your life and taught me the Bible, I'd be damned."

Let me explain a little of the background of her statement. I had started teaching Bible studies in my home years prior to all of this and even though this friend was also a neighbor (and still is), we didn't know each other at that time. One of the ladies in the Bible study invited this particular neighbor to come and join us. She came, and she sat on the fireplace week after week with tears flowing down her precious cheeks as she started to let the balm of scripture heal her heart, broken after her husband walked out on her. (You can read about that situation in "The Final Story" in this book.) As she had rebuilt her family life without her husband, she worked very hard for her money and I know it wasn't easy to let it go, but she did. She was like Jesus, paying a debt she didn't owe so I could go free. She made it possible for me to have something that she never got to enjoy: the privilege of being home again every day with my children, as both their mother and their teacher. Only in eternity will she be paid back for what she has done and has meant to me.

Remember the scripture from Proverbs that says, "The wicked borrow and do not repay"? Well, we didn't have to default on any of our bills; they were all paid. The last part of the scripture passage from Micah 4:10 was now complete—the Lord had redeemed me!

Rick worked late again that same day so I didn't get to tell him about our deliverance until the next morning. God had something beautiful to share with me before I woke Rick up. It was my daily reading from *My Utmost for His Highest*, a collection of the writings of Oswald Chambers (1995). That day's devotion was based on the Scripture passage found in Revelation 3:10, which reads, "Because you have kept My command to persevere . . . ."

> *"Perseverance means more than endurance—more than simply holding on until the end. A saint's life is in the hands of God like a bow and arrow in the hands of an archer. God is aiming at something the saint cannot see, but our Lord continues to stretch and strain, and every once in a while the saint says, "I can't take any more." Yet God pays no attention; He goes on stretching until His purpose is in sight, and then He lets the arrow fly. Entrust yourself to God's hands. Is there something in your life for which you need perseverance*

right now? Maintain your intimate relationship with Jesus Christ through the perseverance of faith. Proclaim as Job did, "Though He slay me, yet will I trust Him" (Job 13:15).

"Faith is not some weak and pitiful emotion, but is strong and vigorous confidence built on the fact that God is holy love. And even though you cannot see Him right now and cannot understand what He is doing, you know Him. *Disaster occurs in your life when you lack the mental composure that comes from establishing yourself on the eternal truth that God is holy love. Faith is the supreme effort of your life—throwing yourself with abandon and total confidence upon God.*

"God ventured His all in Jesus Christ to save us, and now He wants us to venture our all with total abandoned confidence in Him. There are areas in our lives where that faith has not worked in us as yet—places still untouched by the life of God. There were none of those places in Jesus Christ's life, and there are to be none in ours. Jesus prayed, "This is eternal life, that they may know You . . ." (John 17:3). The real meaning of eternal life is a life that can face anything it has to face without wavering. If we will take this view, life will become one great romance—a glorious opportunity of seeing wonderful things all the time. God is disciplining us to get us into this central place of power." (May 8th devotional)

Looking at what that credit card bought me, allow me to paraphrase a popular tv commercial for credit cards:

Seeing what a fraud I was—painful.

Getting pride ripped out of my heart—horrific.

Genuine faith—priceless!

I personalized this portion of 1 Peter into a praise song of my own as an appropriate way to end this story:

"Praise be to the God and Father of my Lord Jesus Christ! By His great mercy He has given me a new birth into a living hope through the resurrection of Jesus Christ from the dead, and into an inheritance that can never perish, spoil or fade—kept in heaven for me, who through faith am shielded by God's power until the coming of the salvation that is ready to be revealed in the last time. In this I greatly rejoice, though now for a little while I may have to suffer grief in all kinds of trials. These have come **so that** my faith—of greater worth than gold, which perishes even though refined by fire—may be proved **genuine** and may result in praise, glory and honor when Jesus Christ is revealed. Though I have not seen Him, I love Him: and even though I do not see Him now, I believe in Him and am **filled** with **inexpressible** and **glorious joy**, for I am receiving the **goal** of my faith, the salvation of my soul." I Peter 1:3-9 (*emphasis mine*)

The Final Story

"Faith without works is dead . . ."

Whew! I can't believe that I'm finally writing the last chapter of this little book. It's been a little over three years since I got what I believed was a word from God to write it. I have written this book amidst hungry kids asking, "What's for supper, Mom? Are you still writing?" I have taught several Bible studies, led a couple of retreats, spoken at local churches, worked a part-time job, and cut friends' hair in the middle of my kitchen, all while still writing this book. So the fact that I am on my final story and that this book has been written at all is a small miracle. I have never had aspirations to be a writer and am not driven to write. I only did this as a labor of love for Jesus Christ.

On the other hand, the truth is that we are all writing a book each and every day of our lives for others to read whether it's penned on paper or not. Listen to what Paul says in 2 Corinthians 3:2-3, "You yourselves are our letter, written on our hearts, known and read by everybody. You show that you are a letter from Christ, the result of our ministry, written not with ink but with the Spirit of the Living God, not on tablets of stone but on tablets of human hearts."

This story involves me and my friend who helped and continues to help me financially. I would say that she is the result of my ministry on one hand, and I have become a result of her ministry on the other. I hope as the above Scripture says that we have both become "letters from Christ that are written on hearts, known and read by everybody." How beautiful the Body of Christ must be to God the Father as we walk in love and work together with no motive but to love Him and each other. I hope we make Him proud.

My friend, who told me not to use her name when I wrote this story, wants all glory and honor for her life to be given to The Living God and not to her flesh. That is a true pinnacle for a child of God because people may give and give generously, but most will receive their reward on earth, and if they're honest, that "earthly reward" is what most people are actually interested in receiving. But listen to what Jesus Himself said in Matthew 6:1-2, "Be careful not to do your 'acts of righteousness' before men, to be seen by them. If you do, you will have no reward from your Father in heaven. So when you give to the needy, do not announce it with trumpets, as the hypocrites do in the synagogues and on the streets, to be honored by men. I tell you the truth, they have received their reward in full." It takes true faith to be generous and remain anonymous, to not work it into conversation somehow and let everyone know what you've done. But when you announce it to the world, all your "gift" truly does is exalt you and actually brings shame and degradation to the needy person. People judge you as the righteous and wonderful one and judge the needy person as someone who is unworthy and needs to get his act together. I've been both the judger and the judged one. God deliver me from judging. Scripture says not to judge or we will be judged the same way. He doesn't pronounce condemnation at all on the judged one. Let others judge me all they want; I just pray that through much humiliation, God has finally started true deliverance for me from passing judgment on others. When we are harsh with others, we need to remember that there are always things about their situation that we don't know. God says that He desires for us to be full of mercy. Until I had to have so much mercy from God for myself, I wasn't very merciful to others. I'm so glad for wounds that God has allowed in my life. I can say with Hezekiah, "I cried like a swift or thrush, I moaned like a mourning dove. My eyes grew weak as I looked to the heavens, I am troubled; O Lord, come to my aid! But what can I say? He has spoken to me and He Himself has done this. I will walk humbly all my years because of this anguish of my soul. O Lord, by such things men live; and my spirit finds life in them too. You restored me to health and let me live. Surely it was for my benefit that I suffered such anguish. In Your love You kept me from the pit of destruction; You have put all my sins behind Your back" (Isaiah 38:14-17).

Anguish of the soul is very powerful and it can either produce humility or hostility. I chose humility and so did my friend.

As you read in "My Most Painful Story," I needed deliverance. I had to be delivered financially or lose everything, materialistically speaking. My friend, on the other hand, needed to be delivered from the fear of not having financial security for her children and herself. Her husband had walked out on all of them and she was left to raise her children without child support or alimony. Although when the events in "My Most Painful Story" took place she had a great job and was amassing an impressive retirement portfolio, her salary wasn't huge when we first met. But after many years at the bottom, she had definitely climbed the cooperate ladder, was in a regional position and was on her way to becoming very comfortable financially.

When her husband first left, she had lots of debt but that wasn't the worst part—she was bitter and heart-broken toward him. She loved him with all of her heart and much of her hope for happiness and a future was wrapped up in him, so when he left, she felt that her hope and future went with him. She didn't realize that as Jeremiah says, "For I know the plans I have for you," declares the LORD, "plans to prosper you and not to harm you, plans to give you hope and a future" (Jeremiah 29:11). God's hope and future for believers are secure, but if our hope is placed in others or money, it can vanish in a day.

God didn't cause her husband to leave her, but He promised in Romans 8:28 that if we love Him, all things will be used for our good and His glory. In the midst of her broken life and heart, my friend started coming to Bible study. She would cry the entire time and always had only one prayer request; "Pray for my children." I've met very few women that love their children as fiercely and loyally as she does. The love she had for those boys kept her from giving up and pressed her toward the healing that only God could bring. She and I became friends and she started to see God doing amazing things in my life. She is the person who insisted that this book be written. Her faith and healing started to grow exponentially. She borrowed cassette tapes of David Jeremiah, Chuck Swindoll, and Greg Laurie and would spend all her driving time just soaking in the Word of God. She got to the place of being able to finish my sentences when I would try to share things from the Word with her; I loved it.

I saw God take her wounded heart and gently replace it with a new heart. I saw that new heart start coursing with forgiveness toward her husband and a new love for him. It was no longer selfish love; it was love that cried out for his salvation. She started to thank God for what happened to them because her focus was now on God and not on a man. That's the only way to truly love another person anyway. If God is not our first love, then all our love for others will turn to hate if they reject us. Watching her get her wobbly legs of freedom underneath her was beautiful.

God started small with her to help her begin to trust Him with her money. When her husband left, she continued her monthly support for a child in Africa. It was a small amount but huge to her. She continued tithing to her local church. God provided money for her son to go on a beach trip when she couldn't afford it. Her trust and faith were slowly building. She helped a mutual friend with a pretty large sum of money when she needed it—another sign that her small faith was growing. Spiritual growth is wonderful, and when the Son sets you free, you will be free indeed. He wants us to look at the future and "laugh at the days to come" (Proverbs 31:25b). He wants us completely free from any love of money. He actually wants us to look at all our money and things as His and not ours on any level. Whew! That's a high order, but one that He can fulfill if we will only let Him. If we only knew the freedom of trusting God, we would hate anything that would threaten to take our hearts away from Him. That's why the Bible can say that if we cling to God we will hate money. I don't think that actually means "hate" as dislike. I think it means "hate" in the same way Luke 14:26 does, "If anyone comes to Me and does not **hate** his father and mother, his wife and children his brothers and sisters—yes, even his own life, he cannot be My disciple." Of course that can't mean we are to hate those people, not in the way we humans define "hatred," but we are to prefer God without contest over them. Our love for them will prove destructive and clingy if we don't love God more. They are safe only as God pours His love through us to them. They will be truly loved then. That is the only way to love money; let God pour through us and use it to bless and help others as an offering to Him.

Since God used the circumstance of divorce to get her heart free from idolatry with a person, He used our circumstance to help set her heart free from the idolatry of clinging to money. The Bible says that if we cling to money then we will hate God. That's because God intends to be our only security, and our sinful nature just naturally wants to cling to something more tangible. None of us can help how we are wired inside and God doesn't judge us for that; He just won't allow us to stay that way since we now have His life in us to defeat all His foes. As He did and continues to do in me, He has done in her; He will leave no stone unturned in our hearts. My friend grew up extremely poor and felt the need to take care of herself from about the tender age of thirteen. She never felt secure and wanted desperately to not have to worry about her future. Those are good qualities unless they are in competition with the life of God in us. As my friend has shared with me since this happened, that was the case for her. She felt that if she didn't have an emergency fund in place at all times for her and her children, disaster would be looming in her future. When she met with me that day, the amount needed to deliver my family from our mess would take her entire savings. Thank goodness she didn't tell me that at the time. I guess I would have just died. Now as we look back, we both see what God was doing, but at the time we were both scared to death for different reasons.

Faith without works is dead—the book of James clearly says that. God had been pouring Himself into her and she was beginning to get to know Him in theory. Now He was taking her to the next step, knowing Him and His provision in reality. You can say you have faith all day in what God can do, but until you step out in obedience, those are just words. When you do what God says, no matter how scared you may be, God gets up and starts to move on your behalf because your actions just said to God, "I believe You and I believe You enough to do what You say!" Listen to what the book of James says, "What good is it, my brothers, if a man claims to have faith but has no deeds? Can such faith save him? Suppose a brother or sister is without clothes and daily food. If one of you says to him, 'Go, I wish you well; keep warm and well fed,' but does nothing about his physical needs, what good is it? In the same way, faith by itself, if it is not accompanied by action, is dead." My friend's faith was proving to be coursing with the life of God.

Scripture says that if we have faith and it is only as big as a mustard seed, we can move mountains. Well, He moved a mountain for her as well as for me. God never wastes anything. She emptied her savings account, by faith, of several thousand dollars! Now, according to her employer, she was due to receive a bonus check that would be almost the same amount as the amount she had just withdrawn, but that money was not in her hand and anything could have happened between emptying and refilling that account. The bottom line was that even after the proposed bonus check arrived, she would still wind up with only the original amount, not the promised double amount. I won't retell the story here since it is in the preceding chapter, but what she did was monumental. She did it for love of God and trying hard to please Him in the midst of insecurity and doubts. And when she got her bonus check, it wasn't for the exact amount that she had given to me. It was actually for **twice** that amount! God wanted to show her that He owns everything and wanted her to see Him, not her bank account, as her source. Just like God chose Abraham to be the vessel to birth a nation that would ultimately give us our Messiah because He knew that he would be faithful, God has chosen to give my friend a "giving" ministry because He knew that she would learn this lesson and she would prove faithful. She is God's steward of His money and He is able to help Himself to her account any time He chooses.

God put Abraham to the ultimate test when He asked him to sacrifice Isaac. Although he was a gift from God, Abraham's heart started to cling to the gift instead of the Giver. God could not let things continue that way because it would defile not only Abraham and Isaac's relationship, but like a cancer, it would spread to every part of Abraham's life. God never wanted Abraham's son; He wanted to make sure He had Abraham's heart so that he could love that boy without clinging to him. When anyone clings to another person, death has started in the relationship. The one who is clung to, will ultimately want to be free. Thank God He wants to be our unrivaled love so that He can pour love through us (so we can be satisfied first) and then to others, so it is not a love that grasps, but a love that gives and is so refreshing that others are drawn to it. To know that we have access to an inexhaustible source is an astounding truth. God gave Isaac right back to Abraham once he no longer had God's place in his heart.

I think that parallels what happened to my friend. When she sacrificed her money to God (remember that we can't fool Him, He knows when it's real), He saw that money left the throne of her heart, so He could now trust her to pour much more money through her open hands. How beautiful! To think that she could have gone through life pouring her attention and love on something so fragile as money would have been an ultimate tragedy. She is now plugged into a source that is both immovable and inexhaustible: God Almighty.

I love what I've heard Bill Stafford say often during sermons, "God will turn hell upside down to meet my needs and make the devil deliver the bucket." That's trust and truth! How silly it must seem to the hosts of heaven as they look upon mankind and see us cling to what we call security, and they then turn and look to the throne and see the glory of God and His offer to give us Himself. They must shake their heads in disbelief and say, "Fools!" We exchange the glory of the Living God for pieces of paper called money. I praise God that He has allowed me to see what He will do with a person that decides to take Him at His Word.

My friend has not only been delivered, but she has gone on to help so many people financially and spiritually in the years since God worked through her to rescue my family from a financial disaster. I know she doesn't think enough about it to even keep track of it by writing it all down. You see, she has reached the place where Jesus always wanted to take her. She paid a high price, but this now describes her, "But when you give to the needy, do not let your left hand know what your right hand is doing, so that your giving may be in secret. Then your Father, who sees what is done in secret, will reward you." (Matthew 6:3-4).

I love you, friend, and I would consider it a high honor to get to hear our Jesus say to you, "Well done, my good and faithful servant! You have been faithful with a few things; I will put you in charge of many things. Come and share in your master's happiness!" (Matthew 25:23).

A Final Note . . .

My Most Painful Story (Bible Study Part of Story)

I often teach that if God allows great suffering into your life and you endure it in faith, you will see His glory in ways that will blow your mind. If He only allowed severe suffering, we would lose heart and if He always gave us glory, we would become proud and selfish. But God is perfect and He always allows the perfect amount of "whatever" in His perfect time.

It has taken me many years to say this—and you may not believe me when I say it—but I love the fact that He allows great suffering in my life. I'm sure I would be very spiritually shallow if I could rebuke Satan and relieve myself of everything that I perceive as negative and painful. God's love is not like mine; He does what is best, not what will make me like Him more. Through suffering, I cry out for more of Him so I can endure it. As a result, I get filled with His Spirit, and I am then able to do what will bring me joy, which is to truly love Him from my heart. I have learned through reading the works of Scottish preacher Oswald Chambers (1995) that the only true lover of God is the Holy Spirit and unless I'm filled with that Holy Spirit, I won't love God.

If you read your Bible and really think about what it says, you will see that a cosmic shift happened when Adam and Eve ate from the tree. After they ate, they were afraid of God, and His presence brought fear, not comfort, to their hearts. They no longer bore His image of perfection. They were full of sin. I don't think we truly understand what Jesus did for us on the cross. We may try so hard to be good. But Jesus didn't die to make us good. Hallelujah! He died to make us righteous. Adam and Eve were innocent, not righteous. The only righteous person to ever inhabit human flesh was Jesus Christ. All other people referred to as "righteous" have borrowed righteousness from the only source of true righteousness—Jesus. One of my favorite scriptures is Luke 1:74b-75, which reads ". . . and to enable us to serve Him without **fear** in **holiness** and **righteousness** before Him **all** our days" (*emphasis mine*). Those words came out of Zechariah's mouth when John the Baptist was born. The Holy Spirit was speaking through Zechariah words that he couldn't have understood at the time. God was speaking through him of a time when He would put mankind back into a right relationship with Himself by making sinners righteous.

When people ask me how I'm doing as I go about my day, I always say something like, "Great" or "Better than I ought to be" and I mean it, because the truth is that I should be in hell, but I'm not. The Bible says that since I am born again, my body is the temple of the Holy Spirit. Are you serious?! The temple in the Old Testament was a place of worship and sacrifice. God's presence was in the Holy of Holies and the high priest could only enter that place one time each year to offer sacrifice for Israel's sins. It would have meant certain death and the height of presumption to go in there any other time. Yet, through the blood of Jesus, I have constant access to the Holy of Holies in my own body. The more that I learn to walk in the light of that truth, the more I find it hard to have a bad day. Job understood something of God's nature to be able, at the announcement of the death of all his children, to worship God in that moment and say, "Naked I came from my mother's womb, and naked I will depart. The LORD gave and the LORD has taken away; may the name of the LORD be praised" (Job 1:21). It has taken me a long time to understand the reason Job could do that. He trusted God. That may sound like a huge over-simplification so I'm going to give you a case in point.

One day, as my son Scott was preparing to go to college, I jokingly told him that I wasn't going to miss him. He looked at me and said, "I would never believe that for one minute no matter what you say." He trusts my heart and never doubts my love for him. Therefore, if I do something he doesn't understand, he doesn't immediately think I'm out to get him or trying to ruin his life. He knows that behind everything

I do concerning him that I have his best interest at heart. Some may think that Scott is displaying a very cocky attitude, acting so sure of my love, but I don't see it that way at all. Scott isn't acting—he is that sure of my love, and that makes me feel like a good mom.

I think that's how God feels when we lift our heads and know that we are loved by Him, no matter what circumstances may look like. Sinning is not the most evil thing I can do. Although most people just assume that it is, the truth is that the most evil thing I can do is doubt God's goodness and love toward me. Committing a terrible sin is a dreadful thing, but all that proves is how weak, needy, helpless, and in need of grace I am. Doubting God's love and goodness makes God out to be a monster in my mind. If I thought my kids suspected me of ill will toward them, it would devastate me much more than a teenage pregnancy, getting kicked out of college, getting drunk, or any other moral lapse or sin you could fill in the blank with. I love them unconditionally and nothing brings me more joy than for them to know that and to walk in that fact, even if they don't understand me or my decisions sometimes.

I learned from many great Christian biographies and from the Bible study "Experiencing God," written by Henry Blackaby (1990), that it is normal for God to speak to and lead His children. As a matter of fact, Blackaby quoted a scripture that I didn't realize was in the Bible. It's Amos 3:7 and it says, "Surely the Sovereign LORD does nothing without revealing His plan to His servants the prophets." If that's true, then as He works in the world, He reveals what He is about to do to His servants. He told Moses His plan to deliver the Hebrews from Pharaoh's power since He intended Moses to be a part of it. He told Abraham what He was going to do to Sodom and Gomorrah before He did. He also told Abraham that the Hebrews would be slaves in Egypt before it ever happened, and I could go on. I started to see that indeed it was normal for God to let you in on what He was doing as He was working in your life. He has a plan and you get to join Him in His plan. He's not just answering your prayers in isolation. He is letting you be a part of His redeeming work on the planet. In other words, it's not all about you and your little corner of the world. In actuality, He is working out a magnificent plan in this vast universe and each of us gets to be part of something so much bigger than we could ever imagine.

The sad thing about that last statement is that most people don't read and study their Bible, so they just walk around in a confused mess for most of their lives. God's plan marches on and He still uses us in spite of ourselves, but we won't enjoy the journey—and believe me when I tell you that you **can** enjoy the journey! Lots of people medicate themselves excessively in an effort to calm their nerves instead of letting the circumstances of life—good and bad—draw them close to the heart and face of The Living God. People do not understand the privilege we possess in having 24/7 access to God Almighty. I don't understand it like I want to, but I draw closer daily with all that is in me.

God is faithful to not only intercede **for** us, but also to pray **through** us to reveal what His will is. So when I was praying for God to give me real love down any road and at any cost, and to make me one with Himself, He was answering. I just didn't understand His ways, so I couldn't comprehend that He was answering. I thought if He would just take away the "heat," then all my yucky feelings would disappear, which would make me feel so much nicer inside, which would make me so much nicer to everyone around me. I'm sure those feelings would have quieted down, but they wouldn't have disappeared. They would have been resurrected every time life threw a curve ball my way. God sees the source or the root of why you do what you do and until that is changed, you will never change. You will just have to work hard to keep your life nice and orderly, making sure that all difficult people are carefully removed. That may mean changing your husband or your wife, your job, not speaking to your children, changing churches—you get the point.

There was a time during the reign of King Saul, when Israel was fighting the Philistines. The story is recounted in the thirteenth chapter of the book of First Samuel, beginning with verse 5: "The Philistines assembled to fight Israel, with three thousand chariots, six thousand charioteers, and soldiers as numerous as the sand on the seashore. They went up and camped at Mikmash, east of Beth Aven. When the Israelites saw that their situation was critical and that their army was hard pressed, they hid in caves and thickets, among the rocks, and in pits and cisterns. Some Hebrews even crossed the Jordan to the land of Gad and Gilead.

Saul remained at Gilgal, and all the troops with him were quaking with fear. He waited seven days, the time set by Samuel; but Samuel did not come to Gilgal, and Saul's men began to scatter. So he said, "Bring me the burnt offering and the fellowship offerings. And Saul offered up the burnt offering. Just as he finished making the offering, Samuel arrived and Saul went out to greet him.

"What have you done?" asked Samuel.

Saul replied, "When I saw that the men were scattering, and that you did not come at the set time, and that the Philistines were assembling at Mikmash, I thought, 'Now the Philistines will come down against me at Gilgal, and I have not sought the LORD'S favor. So I felt compelled to offer the burnt offering."

"You have done a foolish thing," Samuel said. "You have not kept the command the LORD your God gave you; if you had, He would have established your kingdom over Israel for all time. But now your kingdom will not endure; the LORD has sought out a man after His own heart and appointed him leader of his people because you have not kept the LORD'S command."

What I saw in this portion of scripture is that God has certain roles that He has ordained for people. In this case, Saul was the king and not a priest. Although the king was a very important person, he wasn't allowed to take on the role of priest just because he was afraid or thought he knew best. Part of staying within the parameters set for the king was trusting God to take care of what he couldn't. Instead, Saul stepped outside of God's will in an effort to appease God. He thought somehow that God needed His help so they both wouldn't look foolish and defeated. For Saul, serving God was all about keeping rules so he could get what he wanted and not be destroyed, it had nothing to do with trust. He was always looking out for number one, himself. I could really be hard on Saul if I hadn't been afraid, selfish, and tempted to do the same thing, which was to deliver myself. I'm so glad I could read how terribly this turned out for Saul. Since Samuel showed up immediately after Saul had offered the burnt offering, obviously deliverance had been right around the corner, and Saul blew it. I believe it was a test and

Saul failed it miserably. His actions proved that he didn't have faith in God's care and goodness. He stepped outside the boundaries that God had set because God's way wasn't working at least, not in the way and at the speed that Saul wanted. If he couldn't understand how God was going to deliver him, he came to the conclusion that God wasn't going to deliver him at all, so he'd better deliver himself.

Contrast that with Abraham heading up a mountain to sacrifice his son and reasoning that God was going to raise his son from the dead. God had promised Abraham that Isaac was going to be the son through whom He was going to build a great nation, and Abraham's actions showed that he believed that God would keep His word even though he didn't understand how. He even told the servants at the bottom of the mountain that he and Isaac were going to worship God and that **they** would return. What great faith!

God wants our trust and love above anything else. We get so messed up thinking He wants us to always be successful and never make mistakes. We let fear of failure rule our lives. I have truly tried to take to heart the warnings in scripture. In Hebrews 10, the Bible talks about taking to heart what happened during Israel's history. Their unfaithfulness, in spite of God's goodness and faithfulness, was recorded for us, and the Bible even tells us why: "These things happened to them as examples and were written down as warnings for us, on whom the fulfillment of the ages has come. So, if you think you are standing firm, be careful that you don't fall. No temptation has seized you except what is common to man. And God is faithful; He will not let you be tempted beyond what you can bear. But when you are tempted, He will also provide a way out so that you can stand up under it" (1st Corinthians 10:13).

If you've read "My Most Painful Story," then you might remember the quote from Oswald Chambers that I included in that story. It has to do with perseverance and endurance, with maintaining an intimate relationship with Jesus Christ no matter what. That's what the great men and women of the Bible did. That's what the great men and women throughout Christian history have done. That is what I intend to do every day of my life. I pray that you will also. In the end, nothing else will matter.

Even when I am old and gray,
do not forsake me, O God,
till I declare your power
to the next generation,
your might to all who are to come.
Psalm 71:18

References

Alcorn, Randy. (2011). *Safely Home* (3rd ed.), Curtis H.C. Lundgren (Ed). Carol Stream, Illinois: Tyndale House Publishers, Inc.

Blackaby, Henry and King, Claude V. (1990). *Experiencing God Workbook: Knowing and Doing the Will of God.* Nashville, Tennessee: B & H Publishing Group.

Chambers, Oswald. (1995). *My Utmost for His Highest.* James Reimann (Ed), Grand Rapids, Michigan: Discovery House Publishers.

Clark, Dave, Dean Dan, and Koch, Don (Songwriters). (1998). "Mercy Came Running." Universal Music Publishing Group, Warner/ Chappell Music, Inc.

Cowman, Mrs. Charles E. (1965). *Streams in the Desert.* Grand Rapids, Michigan: Zondervan Publishing House.

Marshall, Catherine. (1961). *Something More.* New York: McGraw-Hill Book Co, Inc.

Walsh, Sheila. (1996). *Honestly.* Evelyn Bence (Ed), Grand Rapids, Michigan: Zondervan Publishing House.

25569431R00103

Made in the USA
Lexington, KY
29 August 2013